THE DILF

DAD I'D LIKE TO...FRIEND

HANDBOOK

A NEW DAD'S GUIDE TO OVERCOMING THE MOST COMMON MYTHS OF PARENTHOOD

KEVIN SELDON

The DILF (Dad I'd Like to Friend) Handbook

The events and conversations in this book have been set down to the best of the author's ability, although some names and details have been revised to protect the privacy of individuals.

Copyright © 2023, 2025 by Kevin Seldon

All rights reserved. No part of this book may be reproduced or used in any manner without written permission of the copyright owner except for the use of quotations in a book review.

First paperback edition January 2026

ISBN 978-1-7351605-7-3 (hardback)

ISBN 978-1-7351605-8-0 (paperback)

ISBN 978-1-7351605-9-7 (ebook)

This book was published in partnership with *Dads Supporting Dads*, an arm of 501(c)(3) nonprofit, *All Parents Welcome*.

www.DadsSupportingDads.org

Dad-ication

This book is dedicated to two people:

To my beautifully strong wife and co-parent,
Thank you for making one of my greatest dreams a reality…
and for riding alongside me
on this rollercoaster journey of parenthood.

And to my son,
You have given my life meaning in ways
I never could have imagined.
Thank you for shining bright and reminding me
the true definition of joy.

A Note to Readers

Whether you've just learned you're expecting or your little one has already arrived, welcome to the world of parenthood!

One day (years from now), you'll likely look back at this time as one of the most fulfilling your life had to offer. That said, it's not always easy to pause and appreciate the good times when you're in the thick of it. And it can be even more difficult to step back and see the bigger picture regarding the choices we make (or don't make) as we transition into this next phase of our lives.

You see, there is an endless amount of advice out there once you enter the world of parenthood, and most of that advice will center around your children. However, there are a number of *other* pivotal areas that will significantly impact your experience as a new parent, yet are all too-often ignored.

The fact is, parenthood involves much more than "child-rearing," and those neglected areas are what this book intends to highlight — focusing on three universal themes crucial to *every* parent on the planet:

1. The Significance of Building a Strong Support System
2. How Advocating for *Your* Needs Actually Benefits Your Entire Family
3. Why the Health of Your Relationship with Your Co-Parent* Matters as Much as the Act of Parenting Itself

It should be noted that in lieu of limiting terms like primary or secondary parent, I will use the term "co-parent" quite often throughout this book; however, I define the term a bit differently from some others in the parenting space.

There are many who reserve the term co-parent for situations where a child is being raised by two (or more) people living in separate homes — for example, parents who are divorced, separated or were never together in the first place. In these scenarios, the term is used as *each* parent must individually carry the weight and responsibility of parenthood while working together to create some form of cohesive environment for their child.

In my opinion, reserving this term for those situations is an outdated methodology. Why should two parents need to be living in separate homes for each to share responsibility on the home front?!

For those without a co-parent, please know that regardless of the terminology used, most of the insights offered will still apply. But for those not going at it alone, I think it's about time we update some of the terminology used within the parenting space. Times have changed. Parents come in all forms, and it's rare that there is only one person in a child's life with a vested interest in their upbringing. This book, therefore, will rely on a more inclusive definition of co-parenting — one that involves all parties, each with differing perspectives, learning to come together to create the best environment possible for our kids — no matter your relationship status or living situation.

With that said, let's dive in.

A BIT OF BUSINESS:

- * after a word denotes that the term can be found in the glossary at the end of the book
- Superscript numbers (like this [1]) reference an endnote
- # following a word denotes an associated QR code at the end of the book
- Lastly, please note that this book is for informational purposes only, and is not a substitute for personalized medical advice, diagnosis or treatment

CONTENTS

Introduction		1
Top Myths of Parenthood		9
MYTH #1	MEN HAVE NO INTEREST IN THE UPBRINGING OF THEIR CHILDREN	11
MYTH #2	PATERNITY LEAVE IS UNNECESSARY	37
MYTH #3	YOU WILL FEEL AN INSTANT BOND WITH YOUR BABY	55
MYTH #4	POSTPARTUM DEPRESSION IS NOT A REAL THING	73
MYTH #5	YOU WILL NEVER SLEEP AGAIN	87
MYTH #6	THERE'S NO ROOM FOR MISTAKES AS A PARENT	111
MYTH #7	YOU WILL NEVER HAVE SEX AGAIN	129
MYTH #8	THERE IS ONLY ONE CORRECT WAY TO DO THINGS	153

| MYTH#9 | GOOD PARENTS ALWAYS PUT THEIR KID'S NEEDS FIRST | 171 |
| MYTH#10 | YOU WILL LOVE EVERY MOMENT OF BEING A PARENT | 185 |

QR Resource Guide	198
The DILF Glossary	199
Endnotes	208
About the Author	224

INTRODUCTION

When I first learned I was going to become a dad, I was admittedly in shock. Within a short period of time, though, that shock turned to excitement. But, before I could fully process any of those feelings, I went into panic mode.

After countless pregnancy test disappointments, I was in a bit of disbelief that we had actually achieved our goal — hence, the shock. And after years of build-up, it wasn't *shocking* that excitement would soon follow. However, the panic took me a bit by surprise. I'm not usually one for panic.

But let's back up a bit.

In my professional life, I spent over a decade running my own social-impact consultancy that I launched right out of college — pairing top brands and talent, from NBCUniversal to The Roots, with worthwhile causes like St. Jude Children's Research Hospital and Rock The Vote. In short, my company created projects to bring about positive change in the world. I've produced everything from bi-coastal concert series for

Vanity Fair Magazine to The Roots' annual Pre-Grammy Jam Session. I've dealt with multitudes of demanding clients and stressful situations, and panic never helps to solve the issue at hand. In my experience, panic is most often the result of extreme worry — and as Mark Twain once said, "Worrying is like paying a debt you don't owe. I have spent most of my life worrying about things that have never happened."[1]

Nevertheless, the reality of carrying the weight of responsibility for another human being is a lot to digest. No matter your situation — whether you're hesitant, terrified, or ecstatic — finding out you are going to become a parent can lead to panic. And it's entirely justified.

Now, panic can manifest in many different ways. Some people run (option one) — hopefully only a short distance before they come back to their senses. Others turn on frantic go-mode (option two), while some retreat into their own heads and stop communicating their feelings altogether (option three). The latter is probably the most common for men, which is somewhat understandable, as society often trains us from an early age to push down our feelings and "man up."

I found myself in an odd mix of options two and three — acting as a sleepless problem solver while attempting to ignore any and all of the feelings bubbling up inside of me.

INTRODUCTION

For those of you reading this who might be leaning towards option one (whether still expecting or already with a baby at home), the one thing I ask is that you take the time to finish this book and see how you feel by the end *before* you make any big decisions on how you choose to proceed.

Through years of interviews, research and lived experience, I've found that one of the main roots of panic (particularly in dads) is the substantial lack of resources available regarding our emotional well-being, especially when it comes to starting a family. Another major motivating factor is the lack of support often felt by new parents, which can lead to a surprising emotion that seems at odds with a growing family: isolation.

I, personally, found the road to parenthood extremely isolating, due to my decision to swallow my feelings and focus all of my attention on my partner (in my case, my wife) and our unborn child. Now, I'm not saying that there is anything wrong with focusing a good amount of attention on your family, but I now know that you must also leave some room for yourself, or you'll honestly be no good to anyone — but we'll get more into that later.

For now, I cannot stress enough the importance of finding outlets to express whatever it is you may be feeling. I found a surprising sense of relief after first verbally acknowledging the struggles I was experiencing. You may find that many of those feelings (as well as any associated panic) quickly fade the moment they exit your mouth. Perhaps, they simply require the freedom to be vocalized.

And this is especially the case when it comes to any feelings of isolation, which seem to be so common amongst new parents. As a new dad, I felt left out of the equation at almost every turn. This began from the moment I learned we were expecting. I told a friend, "We're having a baby!" and she responded, "Well, your wife is." And although that may have been factually true, was I not a member of the team? Were we not in this together for the long haul?

This feeling of being left in the cold continued as I was rarely included in conversations regarding the pregnancy and our pending arrival. And I am well aware that I was not the one carrying the baby. But, as someone who was intending to *carry* an equitable share of the responsibility in our child's upbringing, I did find it a bit odd to be sidelined. I also found it difficult to find resources for new dads, except for a few books focused on the logistics of child-rearing while referencing the ineffective mentality of "happy wife, happy life."

INTRODUCTION

The issue with this mentality is that it unjustly implies that the weight of all our emotions should be entirely dependent upon our partner. It also sends the message that we, as dads, are not entitled to any emotional complexity or feelings of our own?!

On the flip side, this very experience was my inspiration in launching a podcast called *DILF (Dad I'd Like To... Friend)*# — focused less on parenting advice and more about creating a safe space that welcomed dads into the parenting fold. The concept was to build an honest and vulnerable forum to express some of my own struggles, while learning from other dads I respected. To share stories of modern parenthood from the often-ignored perspective of a dad. But in honesty, my main goal was to find out if I was alone in all of the feelings I was having.

Spoiler Alert: I was not.

This is the first of a handful of QR codes throughout this book. To listen to *The DILF (Dad I'd Like to Friend)* Podcast, simply aim your phone camera from a slight distance at the image to your left and click on the link that pops up.

It wasn't long before the podcast took off, working to improve the mental health of dads by spreading the message that none of us are alone in any of the feelings we might be experiencing. To my surprise, we broke into Apple's top parenting podcast charts all around the world — we even hit #6 in the US!

However, as our community expanded, I began to identify a number of common threads from new parents entering the scene — a laundry list of parenting myths that no one seemed to be directly addressing.

One of the biggest myths I saw repeated throughout pop culture (and society in general) was the idea that dads are all uninvested, bumbling idiots[2]. According to Dr. Meg Meeker, an advocate for father-inclusive parenting, "In the 1970s and 80s, we began using fathers as the butt of many of our jokes."[3] And from the *National Lampoon's Vacation* movies to *The Simpsons*, the media began cashing in on these comedic tropes.

The problem is, as funny as these portrayals may be, they began to permeate throughout our society so deeply that many now believe these stereotypes to be true. Some even internalize them to the degree that they unconsciously "play the part" to match the broken narrative.

INTRODUCTION

But from the hundreds of dads I've interviewed and interacted with through the years, I found the majority to be extremely capable; albeit sometimes lacking the necessary confidence and tools to aid us as parents — hence the creation of this book. It is my belief that once provided with the resources to support ourselves (and in turn, our partner and child), we are all more than capable to tackle whatever gets thrown our way.

With that said, similar to the podcast, this is *not* a traditional handbook on how to raise your child with dos and don'ts. This book is less about child-rearing and more about YOU.

It's about helping you stay connected: to the people you care about, to your favorite hobbies, to your passions, to your hopes and dreams.

It's a study of how our lives evolve as new parents. How our perspective on the world alters. How our attachment to our professional identity shifts. How our relationships — with our partners and ourselves — transform. And how to find a way through the chaos by building a strong foundation for the road ahead.

Consider this book an ongoing mental health resource for your parenting journey — providing the support and tools needed to become the type of patient, present, actively-engaged dad (and co-parent) *anyone* would love to… friend.

TOP MYTHS OF PARENTHOOD

MYTH #1

MEN HAVE NO INTEREST IN THE UPBRINGING OF THEIR CHILDREN

This myth goes hand-in-hand with another I'm sure you've heard at least once in your life:

 Parenting is a woman's job.

I believe that the absurdity of these myths in our modern world goes without saying. But just to ensure that we are all on the same page, let me throw out one statistic. According to a survey of U.S. parents in the fall of 2022[1], 85% of fathers say being a parent is one of the most important aspects of who they are as a person.

If that's not enough to debunk these myths right off the bat, the fact that you are taking the time to read this right now is proof that both these statements are complete BS. If taking the time to pick up a book like this is not proof that dads have a vested interest in the upbringing of their children, I don't know what is.

Unfortunately, these are still common stereotypes that we all deal with on a regular basis — especially from older generations (from bosses and in-laws to mass media):

 A man's job is to bring home the dough, while a woman's job is to take care of the kids and home.

I will admit, however, that there's a reason these myths have persisted. From an animal kingdom perspective[2], human dads are unusual. We belong to a group of less than six percent of mammal species in which dads not only have an interest, but also play a significant role in caring for their offspring. Of course, the degree of that involvement may differ from home to home, but the fact remains that human dads are unique.

When you think about it from the broader perspective of the animal kingdom, it's not surprising that most of the books out there about pregnancy and parenthood primarily focus on birthing parents* (i.e., those who gave birth to their child).[3] After all, they're the ones growing a baby from scratch and have often taken on the role of primary caregiver for centuries.

However, times are changing, and it's crucial that we also invite non-birthing* parents into the conversation. This includes parents through surrogacy, adoption, blended families and dads, like you — whether you're biologically related to your child or not. But with that invitation comes the responsibility to actually step up and earn this new title of: Parent.

So here it is, your official invite to the party. And the best way to RSVP, as well as combat the dated mentalities mentioned above, is to be the example of what a modern dad is actually capable of. In truth, that might be our only way to transform this broken narrative for future generations.

For many, this may raise questions of *how* to move beyond interest to action when it comes to the upbringing of your children? To put it another way, how can you best engage and earn that title — making yourself an indispensable part of the family equation?

Contrary to popular belief, this process ideally begins prior to the baby even entering the scene. Before we get to that, though, let's discuss the potential elephant in the nursery.

THE GAME OF WHAT-IFS

As mentioned in the introduction, I personally went into panic mode shortly after learning we were expecting, consumed by anxiety and what-ifs. And from all the dads I've interviewed since then, I now know that I was *far* from alone. Without a baby in my belly or any external sign that I would soon become a parent, I found it difficult to connect with what my future would hold. I didn't even feel fully justified in any of the anxieties I was experiencing. They almost felt selfish. I thought to myself.

 You are not allowed to have any feelings right now. Your sole focus should be on your pregnant partner and unborn child.

This was another myth that took its toll on my mental health. In response, I pushed down my feelings — unaware that this would only make everything I was feeling more intense. Worse, it would eventually affect everyone around me.

For those whose journey does not involve pregnancy, like adoptive or LGBTQ+ dads, the emotional transition can be just as intense. The truth is that no matter your situation or how you become a parent (for instance, if you got your partner pregnant, if you two are no longer/never were together, if you became a parent through surrogacy or adoption, or if you married someone with children), there is nothing wrong with you if you are experiencing panic or anxiety. I really cannot express this enough. In fact, it's much more common than most realize. But that doesn't mean you cannot do anything about it.

One Harvard study[4] recommends a great technique: relabeling anxiety as… excitement. The study[5] discusses how these two emotions are physiologically similar, and how a slight shift in perspective can be extremely beneficial. In other words, simply reframing the emotion in a more positive context (in our minds, as well as in conversation) can change the way we think, which can, in turn, change the way we feel.

Here's an example of relabeling with a thought that has crept into the minds of most expectant parents at least once:

> *"I'm anxious about becoming a parent. What if I suck at this?!"*

Now, here's the reframed version of the same sentiment with a more positive spin:

> *"I'm excited to see what it's like to become a parent. I hope I do a good job."*

The latter statement is just a bit easier to digest, no? It leaves the door open to do the work to become the type of parent you want to be.

Of course sometimes, anxiety can become debilitating (we'll touch on this more in Myth #4), and in those cases, it's important to seek out assistance from a licensed healthcare professional. But in situations where anxiety is present but not consuming, think about it like this: if you're anxious about something, it often means that you care about the outcome, and you (like most people) likely want it to work out well. There's nothing wrong with that. To me, that sounds a lot like *excitement*.

Unfortunately, the negative side of excitement (i.e., anxiety) can sometimes prevent us from putting our best foot forward, which is why I suggest finding ways to channel that energy into something positive and productive. Lucky for you, that's what this chapter is all about.

Since anxiety is often associated with feeling a lack of control[6] over any given situation, one of the best ways to calm our minds is to take action. As a professional producer, one of the first lessons I learned is that nothing diminishes panic quicker than action. Even a few tiny steps in the right direction can significantly reduce any feelings of anxiety by putting you back in the driver's seat. It can help boost your confidence without the risk of overwhelming you.

That's precisely what helped me. I reframed the perinatal* period (the time from learning you are going to be a parent and continuing up to roughly one year following the birth of your child) as a time to get prepared for what was to come, as well as get on the same page as my parenting co-pilot. I focused on the small actions I *could* take, rather than the multitude of things I had absolutely no control over. Not only did taking action calm my anxieties during that strenuous time, it also still works for me to this day.

BABY STEPS

Although much of this book will apply no matter where you find yourself in your parenting story, let's begin with the time period leading up to your baby's arrival... and one of the most common myths regularly believed by the masses:

 There's not much for dads to do during the pregnancy.

The truth is that there is *so* much you can do to prepare yourself. To clarify, I am not talking about those lists mentioned in the majority of baby books out there, like being your partner's masseur or personal cravings concierge. These are excellent ways to support a pregnant partner and help alleviate *their* stress, but they should go hand-in-hand with the following actions that can also help to better prepare *you* for the adventures ahead.

1. Baby Talk

During pregnancy, there are two ways to communicate with your baby. Yes, you read that right. There are two ways to bond with your little one prior to birth, and both fall into a category known as prenatal* (prior to birth) bonding.

MYTH #1 – MEN HAVE NO INTEREST IN THE UPBRINGING OF THEIR CHILDREN

Although some may argue that babies don't yet have the ability to bond with anyone while still in the womb (despite studies suggesting otherwise), those making that argument may be missing the point.[7]

Again, the not-so-hidden motivation behind this book is to better support *you* as you transition into your new role as a parent. Beyond the multiple potential benefits for your unborn child, the simple act of communicating with your little one during pregnancy can assist you in visualizing what it will be like once they enter the world. That mental shift alone can help you bond more easily with your baby upon arrival.

Prenatal Bonding: Direct Contact

This first option involves those who have physical access to the birthing parent's baby bump. If you fall into this category, any interactions with that growing belly will likely assist you in feeling a strong connection with your child.

Take the time to touch the baby bump (with prior approval, of course) and talk about all the things you are doing to get ready for their arrival. Make the time to read, or even sing to them. Introduce them to the family they are being born into. Share all the things you're excited to do together once they arrive. Utilize this brief moment in time to allow your new identity as a parent to sink in.

This will also offer the first major opportunity to build a united front* with your co-parent... depending on the words you use. Early on, I found myself saying things to my partner's belly like, "Daddy loves you and can't wait to meet you." I then began to notice my partner making statements like, "Mommy loves you, and can't wait to meet you."

On the surface, there's nothing wrong with either of these statements. They both begin the process of helping you to connect with your baby. Although, I must honestly admit that I did notice the beginnings of a bad habit forming. Almost like a subtle amount of silent competition for the affection of our little one. And this may not be an issue for everyone. But, I did feel an energy shift whenever I rephrased my language to include my partner. Even just a small tweak — "Daddy loves you *and* your mommy so much" or "*We* are so excited to meet you!" — made a big difference. Before long, I noticed my wife using more "we" statements, which immediately made me feel like someone had my back.

It may seem like a small thing, but I highly recommend thinking about this when speaking to your child — both before and after birth. Language plays a huge part in strengthening bonds and making two individuals feel like a team. And that is one of the main goals of this book: to help you build a united front with your co-parent that will stand the test of time.

Prenatal Bonding: Direct Mail

The second way to communicate with your unborn child — whether or not you have access to the baby bump — is to write them a letter. You can grab a notebook and begin journaling or create an email account using the baby's name as soon as you have it finalized. You can even include mementos (from shower invites to sonograms) as keepsakes for the day your kid is old enough to appreciate them.

I mean, is it ever too soon to start creating memories?!

You can write monthly letters leading up to the birth or simply write a short note whenever you're moved to do so. And you can continue this tradition after the birth as often as you see fit. You can also give the email address to close family and friends to send letters when your baby is born, and if desired, on every birthday that follows. I personally love that my son will one day be able to read letters from his grandparents — even if they may no longer be with us.

Aside from creating an ever-evolving time capsule for your child, this will also provide the added benefit of allowing you the space to acknowledge all you have to be grateful for. In fact, the simple act of practicing gratitude has been scientifically proven[8] to improve both your mental and physical well-being, which will be essential for your new role as a dad.

No matter what approach you take, know that any attempts to communicate with your little one prior to birth will provide a powerful opportunity to begin getting comfortable with your new identity as a parent.

2. Babymoon

You've probably heard of this celebrated ritual (similar to a honeymoon) of taking a trip with your partner prior to the birth of your child. This tradition can offer another meaningful opportunity for prenatal bonding, but instead of bonding with your unborn child, the focus is on bonding with your co-parent. I'm a big fan of this ritual (which will mostly only apply to those in a relationship with their co-parent), but know this: you do not have to break the bank to take part. The point is not where you go (you can even do a staycation), it's about creating a moment in time to pause and simply appreciate one another.

It's a time to dream big and get on the same page regarding your hopes for the future. A time to clear your mind, relax, and connect without the chaos of work or other distractions. It's about intentionally choosing to put your relationship above the stresses of the outside world — a skill that will be crucial once a baby enters the scene.

That said, I'm also a big proponent of gamifying intimidating tasks by dangling a reward for myself at the end. In this case, your babymoon. By that, I mean use the anticipation of this responsibility-free time off as the motivation to get any needed baby prep out of the way.

You can start by creating a master list of essential to-dos *with* your partner in preparation for the arrival of your little one. Then, take the time to divide up ownership of those to-dos. The goal is for you each to have tasks you are independently responsible for accomplishing prior to your upcoming getaway.

One thing that might be helpful is getting familiar with a concept too-rarely discussed with most dads (and parents in general). The term mental load* will come up a lot in the following chapters. Introduced by French sociologist Monique Haicault[9] in 1984, the term refers to the weight that comes with all the invisible work necessary to manage one's life. And once a baby enters the picture, that work expands exponentially. It takes a lot of planning and coordinating to keep a household and family running smoothly.

Once the baby arrives, rushing out to replenish diapers when needed, or doing the laundry and dishes, is a great way to carry your share of the physical load. But, helping to carry the mental load involves checking to see if you are running low on diapers and going out to grab more *prior* to running out. It's about doing the dishes and laundry *before* they pile up and someone makes a comment about it.

To further clarify, it's not about asking what you can do or taking orders — that still puts the weight of the mental load on the parent assigning the task. It's about taking ownership of ways you can alleviate some of the weight from your co-parent's shoulders... with the added benefit of proving to yourself just how capable you are on the home front. It's also a great way to build a strong foundation of mutual trust.

For now, just know that the work of sharing the mental load as parents should begin the moment you learn you're expecting. The book *Fairplay* by Eve Rodsky did a lot to raise awareness for the term mental load, and its companion card deck is a great resource for identifying a master list of tasks to review. But priorities differ from home to home. That said, the sooner you and your co-parent create a list of to-dos that you deem necessary and divide them up, the better off you'll be. I like to call this your *Scope of Work** (SOW).

Think about it like this: when any freelancer begins a new gig, they typically sign a contract detailing the agreed-upon tasks they'll be responsible for throughout the course of the project (aka a SOW). Similarly, it's a great idea for you and your co-parent to create a short SOW — divvying up tasks (and the mental load associated with those tasks) however you two see fit. The goal is to set a precedent of shared responsibility within your home.

This isn't about splitting things 50/50, it's more about beginning the conversation and listening to one another's needs. It's about finding a balance that feels right for your family. None of what you decide needs to be set in stone. It's more about laying the groundwork and trying on different tasks to see what fits. It's about learning to work as a team. And once you get some of those tasks out of the way, your babymoon is the perfect time to celebrate all that hard-earned teamwork.

3. Be Your Own Dadvocate

In addition to prenatal bonding (both with your unborn child and your co-parent), there are also a number of studies that show that engaging in prenatal care is a powerful way to help set dads up for success.[10]

According to *DILF* podcast guest Kevin Shafer,[11] Associate Professor of Sociology with a focus on dads at Brigham Young University, "Dads who are actively included in prenatal care form a stronger 'father' identity for themselves."[12] Again, becoming a parent is a big transition, and the sooner you begin to acknowledge the realities of this life change, the better prepared you will be for whatever gets thrown your way.

Getting involved in the prenatal care of your unborn child can include actions like accompanying a pregnant partner to anything from prenatal checkups to ultrasounds — often an expectant dad's first opportunity to experience the reality and excitement of fatherhood. For dads via surrogacy or adoption, attending agency/clinic visits or engaging in legal/medical prep can serve a similar role.

What is often *not* mentioned is that expectant dads can sometimes unfortunately be actively excluded from prenatal care — ignored by doctors and parenting culture in general.[13,14]

Please do not let that stop you.

You may not be carrying the baby in your belly, but you are going to be an active part of this baby's world, so the sooner you get involved, the better! If there is only one thing you get from this chapter, I hope it's this: you must be your own advocate when it comes to your involvement in your child's life.

Being your own advocate means that prior to the arrival of your little one (and continuing throughout your parenting journey), you must continue to show up — even when you don't feel invited. You must fight for your right to be part of the conversation. You deserve the space to voice your opinions and ask questions, but you must speak up.

To clarify, that does not mean that you should be combative or dismissive of those around you. Being your own advocate is a delicate balance of listening to your own needs, while also being respectful of others (specifically, your co-parent).

As this book was written to better support dads, I like to use the term dadvocate* to refer to anyone who advocates for dads to be actively-involved in the family unit (and that includes any dad advocating for themselves). And one of the keys to successfully becoming your own dadvocate is to educate yourself. If you want a seat at the table, you need to at least try to know what you're talking about. This begins with doing your research, which includes taking the time to listen to any wisdom offered — be it from doctors, nurses, doulas or other parents. Never let pride or ego prevent you from hearing crucial intel that can help you and your family to thrive.

> **Dad Shower**
>
> As one of your first official acts in becoming your own dadvocate, why not invite a few dads you respect for a simple pre-baby hang. No gifts necessary. All you ask is for each to bring one piece of advice or some words of encouragement for the journey ahead!

You should also make the time to get familiar with the array of baby gear that will soon fill your home (something too few dads are encouraged to do). Researching and even discovering some new items to make your life easier is a great opportunity to alleviate some of your co-parent's mental load. Plus, the more informed you are regarding recommended must-haves for new parents[#], the better prepared you'll be to use them when the need arises.

But all this begins with making the choice to step up to the plate.

> #To view a product list of New Dad Favorites, use the QR code below:
>
>

4. Build Your Support System

I've saved one of the most crucial (and for some, the most challenging) pieces of the puzzle for last. One of the most overlooked aspects of parenthood is the importance of taking care of *you* — both prior to the arrival of your little one and throughout your adventures as a parent.

Expanding on the concept of being your own dadvocate, you must find ways to advocate for your own needs. You can not expect your co-parent (or anyone for that matter) to be a mind-reader. And there is little chance of you being a strong and stable pillar of support for your family if you are struggling. In fact, being able to recognize when help is needed — and having the courage to ask for it — is one of the most beneficial lessons you can model for your child.

This is where a strong support system* comes into play.

Unfortunately, it's not always easy for men to ask for help, or, if we're being honest, to even forge new close friendships — hence, the modern prevalence of the term "friendship recession." The Survey Center on American Life says that the percentage of men with at least six close friends has fallen by half since 1990, from 55% to 27%, while 15% say they have no close friends at all.[15]

Now, you may be reading this and saying to yourself, *I have tons of friends.* But the question you should be asking yourself is, how many of your friends are you comfortable revealing any vulnerabilities to?

The fact is, it's not always easy to find people you can let loose and laugh with, who also make you feel supported and heard. If you've never seen the movie *I Love You, Man* with Paul Rudd, you should. It's highly underrated, and a great representation of the struggles many of us experience forming strong male friendships. One of the most powerful messages of the film is that although it may take time, if you keep at it (while remaining open to all available options), you *will* find your people.

> #To help in building out your support system, check out DADS SUPPORTING DADS:
>
>

And if you're thinking to yourself, *no thank you*, or that you don't need a support system, please know that pretending you have all the answers in any given situation truly helps no one — least of all you.

Although a strong support system should include your co-parent, know that (contrary to popular belief by many men) this weight may be too much for your partner to carry all on their own, especially once a baby enters the picture. And as your co-parent may likely have fears of their own that they're grappling with, additional support *will* be needed.

Your support system should include a support network of friends, family, and maybe even a therapist. Additionally, I'd recommend an in-person support group of other parents (feel free to check out DadsSupportingDads.org#, which is part of the nonprofit that published this book). It could also include something I like to call an *Invisible Support System**, which includes resources like podcasts, books, inspiring playlists, or online communities — anywhere you can turn, if and when help is needed. The benefits will be undeniable: helping you through any difficult times that may arise, while assisting you to be the best version of yourself for your impressionable little one.

My First Dad Friend

One of my earliest *DILF* interviews was with my first dad friend, whom I met through a set-up by our wives — a sort-of "blind dad date," if you will. A woman posted in her Facebook moms group about her husband seeking some dad friends, and my wife replied, "He should meet mine!" At first, we cordially texted back and forth, but I was playing it cool by waiting a few days to respond, and then texting, "Hey, we should hang sometime" without really specifying a date or time... which got us nowhere.

The truth is, I was a bit nervous. I was already having trouble admitting that I needed support (even though everyone does), but add to that the awkwardness of this "blind date" set up. Then I thought to myself, *What am I doing? This is just an opportunity to hang with another dad. You need this!*

MYTH#1 – MEN HAVE NO INTEREST IN THE UPBRINGING OF THEIR CHILDREN

So I wrote (in what felt like an extremely vulnerable message at the time): "Just wanted to apologize for being so flaky these past few weeks, but would truly love to meet up at some point." It's funny, looking back, how simply adding the word "truly" felt like I was putting myself on the line for rejection, but he ended up writing back immediately. That week, we met up for lunch with our little ones. And he's now one of my closest dad friends, who has helped me through countless tough times.[16]

When in doubt, remember that if you have no support for yourself, it's tough to be of support to anyone else. Remaining open and acknowledging that you might need help from time to time is vital to setting yourself up for success as a parent. The one thing I can guarantee is that whatever you are feeling, you are not alone.

IN CLOSING

Obviously, how you choose to spend your time prior to the birth of your baby (and beyond) is up to you. In my experience, this time is best spent taking baby steps to help you get used to this new role you've been gifted. A time to lay the foundation of a true partnership with your co-parent. A time to build the most calm and loving environment possible for your new addition. A time to learn how to be your own dadvocate and step up to the plate as the best version of yourself.

One of my most referenced quotes regarding fatherhood comes from Pope Francis, who said:

> *"Fathers are not born but made. A man does not become a father simply by bringing a child into the world, but by taking up the responsibility to care for that child."*[17]

In short, the title of parent belongs to those who actively rise to the occasion.

The good news is that when it comes to parenthood, there's a multitude of ways to get involved — the question is:

Will you make the effort to take advantage of them?

MYTH #2

PATERNITY LEAVE IS UNNECESSARY

If you're presently on paternity leave or have plans to take one, then you already know how important this time can be. According to the 2023 U.S Census Bureau, paternity leave* for new dads is up 183% from 2018.[1] However, there are many who still question the significance of taking some dedicated time off after the arrival of a new baby. The following are what I've found to be the three top reasons for not taking paternity leave:

1. My company doesn't offer it, or I can't afford to take unpaid leave.

2. It was offered, but anyone who takes advantage of it is looked down upon.

3. I am self-employed and control my own schedule or I didn't feel the time off was necessary.

If you fall into the first category and your present employer does not offer paternity leave or you can't afford to take it, no one knows your personal financial situation better than you — and although that does not negate the many benefits that paternity leave can provide[2], I completely get it. Hopefully, paid family leave will become a global right in the very near future. Nevertheless, there are still a number of pivotal actions you can take after your baby's arrival, which we'll explore in the next section of this chapter.

On the other hand, if paternity leave *is* an option for you and you are hesitant to take advantage of it, please consider the following: As a society (especially in the U.S.), we have a corporate culture that rarely places a high priority on responsibilities outside of the workplace. And unfortunately, that often translates to work pressures that push new dads into traditional "breadwinner" roles, without much ownership or caregiving responsibilities on the home front.[3] According to an article in the *Harvard Business Review*:

> "Of the fathers who do take paid leave (if it's offered), 70% return to work in 10 days or less, according to the U.S. Department of Labor. A key reason why? Unsupportive leadership. In a 2019 study by the Boston College Center for Work and Family, 55% of men said they didn't feel extremely

MYTH #2 – PATERNITY LEAVE IS UNNECESSARY

supported by senior management in their decision to take paternity leave."[4]

And those pressures continue even for those at the top. A CEO was quoted within the same piece mentioned above, confessing: "The day my twin sons were born was the happiest of my life. There is one thing I regret, though: the conference call I was wrapping up with my executive team as I raced through the hospital doors."

As difficult as it may seem to prioritize your personal life, do not be fooled — you do have a choice in the matter. It is completely understood (and often expected) that one must work hard to provide for their family — there's a reason many say that money makes the world go round. It's also completely justified to care about building your professional legacy. However, it may not be the best idea to prioritize those things over your family, your happiness, or your personal well-being. Again, you *must* be your own advocate!

As the old saying goes, *You teach people how to treat you*. It's not always easy to set boundaries or manage expectations (especially on the workfront), but if you don't, you may soon find yourself in a job — and a life — you no longer enjoy.

Taking advantage of some dedicated time off can set a precedent that your family is *also* a priority — heck, you might even set the tone for your company to realign *their* priorities. And if you need some ammo to back you up, know that research shows that becoming a parent can actually make you more productive and efficient — often due to a necessary reorganization of priorities and improved time management skills.[5] In addition, providing more support to parents has been shown to increase loyalty and retention of high-value employees, while improving productivity and engagement. A recent study by Harvard Business School found that companies who address their employees' caregiving needs reduce absenteeism by up to 50% and achieve a return on investment (ROI) of up to 72%.[6]

For dads where the opportunity to take paternity leave is an option, know that it doesn't have to be an all-or-nothing mentality. You could take leave at the same time as your co-parent to better support each other during those first three months following the birth of your child (often referred to as the fourth trimester*). You could also stagger any available leave — allowing more time without the need for an external caregiver (e.g. nanny, daycare, etc), while guaranteeing more one-on-one time with your new addition. In fact, one study found that dads who took some dedicated time off had closer relationships with their children that lasted well into early adolescence.[7]

You see, when you become a parent, you're in essence taking on an additional job — albeit an unpaid one. Because truth

MYTH #2 — PATERNITY LEAVE IS UNNECESSARY

be told, there are no "non-working parents." *Every* parent works. The only difference is whether or not you're being paid for your time. Unfortunately, unpaid labor does not often receive the respect it deserves, but make no mistake, it's still work. And doesn't any new job — especially one that involves the care of another individual — require an adjustment period?

Parental leave* (which incorporates both paternity and maternity leave) is exactly that — time to get used to this new job title and the responsibilities that come along with it. Like any new job, taking the time to work out all the kinks guarantees an easier transition, and as discussed in Myth #1, creates more room to enjoy this new position you've been gifted.

One thing that may be helpful to remember is that you will very likely not be in the same paid job ten years from now, but you will (hopefully) still have your family. So doesn't it make sense that your family should — whenever able — receive as much, if not more, of your attention as any paid job?

I know some of you may be thinking, *I can't risk my job security. I need to prioritize my career in order to provide for my family!* That is completely understandable, but the fantasy that life can continue just as it did prior to having a baby is simply unrealistic — as if the life-altering addition of another human permanently entering your home won't change a thing? I think we all know better. Similarly, the mentality that the weight of caregiving responsibility should solely lie on your partner (who potentially just gave birth) is a problematic road to go down for everyone involved.

I once had a dad in one of my new-dad groups who was laid off right around the time his partner gave birth. He therefore felt no need to take any "time off" as he was now in complete control over his schedule. The problem was that he spent very little of his time during those first few months focusing on his co-parent *or* his newborn baby.

He was justifiably stressed. He spent most of our time together talking about the array of jobs he'd been applying for. Even though his co-parent was on a paid maternity leave, I get why he was consumed. Life (especially with a baby) is expensive. But it goes beyond that. A 2025 study shows that 86% of men still believe their worth is tied to being a "provider" — associating their professional success as a measure of their overall value[8]. However, as true as that may often feel, it is simply *not* the case.

So, when it came time for his co-parent to go back to the office, I asked if he'd be open to taking two weeks off from the job hunt to focus his attention on the new addition to his family, as well as supporting his co-parent's transition back to work. Easier said than done, but he hesitantly agreed.

When I next saw him, he was a different man. He had allowed himself a break from the grind of the job search and discovered the joy of being a parent. All he could talk about was this amazing relationship he had begun to form with his baby — who'd been there all along, but he had yet to take the time to truly connect with. He was also feeling much more connected to his co-parent, which made parenting a much more enjoyable experience. After a few weeks off (and a newfound perspective), he reentered the job market and quickly found a gig that fit the bill. In short, he was noticeably changed for the better, having taken the time to better support his family and bond with his little one.

For some, the loss of a job can even be the impetus for a life transition. When a salary is less than the cost of childcare — or when a parent is simply miserable in their current career —there may be a great opportunity for that parent to stay home and take on more of the caregiver responsibilities, even if it's only a temporary situation. And there's no reason for that decision to be based on gender. According to the Pew Research Center, the number of Stay-at Home dads within the US and beyond is only growing, with an estimated 2.1 million stay-at-home dads in 2021, up from 1.1 million in 1989.[9,10]

No matter your situation, though, it's important to recognize that the first few months of a baby's life are not simply a dreamy bonding period. The fourth trimester can offer beautiful, serene moments, but it can also feel extremely exhausting and overwhelming. For those thinking that any dedicated time off is unnecessary, as taking care of a newborn can't be that complicated, you are missing some key information.

TEAMWORK

Regardless if you take any parental leave, you should know that the two most important jobs you have when your baby first arrives each come down to the same thing: *survival*.

Of course, there's the vital job of keeping your newborn safe and sound. Rocking them, feeding them, changing them — you'll do this last one *a lot* since babies are like funnels that quickly release whatever they take in after taking out the needed nutrients (yeah, I know my sh*t). However, there's an equally important job that is rarely discussed:

The survival of your relationship with your co-parent

The *New York Times* recently published an article arguing how important parental leave can be for both mothers *and* fathers, not just for bonding with your baby, but also for the well-being of your relationship with your co-parent.[11] The article states that "among 6,000 couples followed from when their child was a baby until kindergarten age, couples in which fathers took even just a week or two of paternity leave were 26 percent more likely to stay married, compared with couples in which fathers took no leave."[12]

This is not that shocking when you think about how stressful the fourth trimester can be for new parents.[13] Being locked inside with your baby, with no other support system available, can lead to intense feelings of isolation, anxiety, or worse. Which is why it's so important to find ways to support one another, whether you officially take parental leave or not.

Making some dedicated time for your family during these first few months not only helps you to adapt to this new normal, but allows you time to adjust to this new relationship dynamic with your co-parent.

It's a time to learn how to best communicate with all of the new responsibilities that now fall on your plate. It's a time to figure out how to work in shifts — allowing you each the opportunity to take a shower, eat hot food, or even go to the bathroom… alone (which is harder than you may think once a baby enters the picture). A time to establish necessary boundaries, so you even feel safe asking for a break when needed — which is not only crucial to the health of your relationship, but also your own physical and mental well-being.

As previously mentioned, it's never too soon to find ways to have one another's back and share that mental load. The first few months are a great time to explore the multitude of ways to create a balance of responsibilities that feels right for your family. If you haven't each settled on your Scope of Work, you can simply begin by digging into any necessary tasks around the house. This could include anything from catching up on laundry or the dishes to preparing bottles. Even just making sure you and your co-parent get the food and hydration you need to keep going.

Just remember that it should never be a game of "tit-for-tat." It's not about splitting tasks evenly. There will always be ebbs and flows in any successful co-parenting relationship. It's about creating a balance that feels right for each of your individual needs and capacities at that specific moment in time. It's about each of you feeling supported, while establishing your ability to handle any tasks that need to get done (without any assistance from your co-parent). And honestly, the sooner you each change a diaper by yourself and handle bath time all by your lonesome, the better off you'll be.

Sleep Support

Another major way to have each other's back is sleep support. The truth is that every baby is unique, which means there's rarely a universal answer to anything, especially when it comes to finding the perfect sleep schedule. But there is one general standard: newborns (babies up to around 3 months old) rarely sleep through the night without *at least* one feeding. Whether or not your co-parent is breastfeeding, this can become quite exhausting.

Additionally, if your co-parent gave birth, their body is likely more exhausted than yours and requires as much time to heal as possible. In this scenario, one of your most important jobs during the fourth trimester is finding ways to allow them time to rest, and in some cases, convincing them that it's okay to accept help.

That is why, if able, I recommend dads try to handle the night shift as much as possible, which could include everything from bedtime routine to any late night feeds (which is, admittedly, much easier if on parental leave). And if weeknights are not a possibility for you, there's always weekends — *any* opportunity to take the baby off your co-parent's hands for an extended period of time.

If budget allows, there's also the option to hire a newborn care specialist* to focus on the needs of the baby, or a postpartum doula* to focus more on the needs of the family, including the parents. However, this option does not eliminate the need (as well as the *many* benefits) to share feeding responsibilities with your co-parent, no matter the time of day.

Co-Feeding

Let me start by saying that although breastfeeding is a preferred option for many birthing moms, it is not the only option. And for those where breastfeeding is not an option, using formula makes the concept of *Co-Feeding** very easy to implement — and can offer many benefits.[14]

To clarify, similar to my modern usage of the term co-parent, my definition of "Co-Feeding" involves more than one individual sharing feeding responsibilities, regardless of where the milk comes from. This is different from the concept of combination feeding* (AKA mixed feeding), which is when you feed your baby a mix of both breastmilk and infant formula.

One recent study showed that many fathers only felt they became a *true* parent after beginning the process of Co-Feeding,[15] which is precisely what happened with me.

My wife breastfed our son, but in an attempt to Co-Feed around a month in, I asked if she would be willing to pump on occasion, which is not always the preference for new moms — my wife in particular. The reason was simple: it's exhausting, uncomfortable, and inconvenient. Obviously, the final decision was not mine to make. But, if she was willing, I could then fully cover the night feeds — allowing her some much-deserved time off, while giving me some much-needed bonding time.

Ultimately, my wife did make the choice to begin pumping before bed, which allowed her to get a full night's sleep. I then took on the entire night shift, which included any feeds that arose during that time period. And I cannot express enough how much it truly benefited the both of us.

This same situation occurred for many of the fathers in the new-dad groups I've led. I will never forget the look on the face of one of my new dads after his co-parent decided to add some pumping into the mix. He had been attempting to handle the night shift, but would then wake his co-parent when it was time for a feed — so, neither of them were getting a good night's sleep.

But after adding some bottles into the mix, he came to class with this glow, after only one week of fully handling the night shift. He no longer felt tethered to his breastfeeding co-parent in order to achieve some quality bonding time with his baby. For the first time in almost three months as a new dad, he finally felt he could truly contribute, and discovered this newfound bond with his little one.

And his co-parent was grateful for the much-needed support and rest. Of course, it was tough on occasion. Sometimes she woke up in the middle of the night full of milk and needed to pump (and it might have seemed easier to simply breastfeed in that moment), but it also gave them the chance to get ahead a bottle. Most importantly, it helped to create more of an equal balance in their co-parenting relationship, one that he recently told me still benefits them to this day.

If you find yourself in a similar situation, note that it helps to learn how to take apart, clean, and reassemble a breast pump (which includes cleaning any associated tubes and bottles) to make this process a bit more manageable for your co-parent. Trust me when I say that if your co-parent is open to it, you will *both* benefit from a Co-Feeding scenario, so any additional time put in to make this a reality is well worth the effort.

And note that Co-Feeding is equally beneficial for dads through surrogacy or adoption using donor milk, formula or a mix of both. What matters is shared responsibility with your co-parent, not the milk source. But like much of parenting, it often comes down to your unique situation.

Whether using breastmilk or formula, just know that a study of over 1,000 parents of children aged six months to five years showed that, without the baby having grown in our bellies, two-thirds of new dads (potentially even more, as men aren't always known to reveal what's going on beneath the surface, especially during a random survey) admit to feeling "left out" in the early days of parenting. That same study showed that a further 83% of fathers said that "feeding their baby was their favorite part of the day."[16]

The study also showed that six in ten of all parents sharing feeding responsibilities (regardless of what time of day that feed occurred), claimed it helped improve their relationship with their co-parent. Many felt closer to one another as a result. And eight in ten fathers even had a newfound appreciation for their co-parent.

Lastly, that same study revealed that the majority of parents (85%) felt that experiencing these small, daily feeding moments were what matters most when developing a bond with your baby. "Bonding is a process and is often the by-product of everyday caregiving," says psychologist Emma Kenny.[17]

In short, the more actively involved each of you are early on, the more connected you will each feel to your baby. But that requires each of you to be present — both physically and emotionally.

IN CLOSING

Whether or not you formally take time off, setting aside some dedicated time after the arrival of your little one can offer innumerable benefits. And it doesn't matter what your family looks like. Whether your partner gave birth, or your baby arrived via surrogate or adoption, every parent deserves the space to adjust to this next phase of their life. It's a time to create routines and make decisions about how you want to level the playing field regarding responsibilities in your home. It's also a time that you will rarely regret having taken advantage of.

> As Winston Churchill once said, "We make a living by what we get. We make a life by what we give."[18]

Think about it this way — your career is not likely to offer you comfort while lying on your deathbed, but your family will. And although the unpaid job of being a parent will admittedly be a lot of work, it will also be one of the most meaningful and fulfilling jobs you'll ever take on.

MYTH #3

YOU WILL FEEL AN INSTANT BOND WITH YOUR BABY

The truth is that you may feel an instant bond with your little one, but you also may not. I didn't. Even if you began reading this book prior to the birth of your baby, and followed every one of the suggested actions provided in the previous two chapters, you still may struggle with forming an "instant" connection with your new arrival. And there's no shame in that — a good amount of people don't feel a bond instantaneously. But that doesn't mean it won't eventually come.

One of the most underrated words you can add to your vocabulary as a new parent is: *yet*.

A dad friend once told me he was raised to believe that Y.E.T stands for "You're Eligible To" — which really stuck with me. The power of that word on the psyche is undeniable. The simple addition of "yet" to any sentence expressing a concern can magically fill the glass from half-empty to half-full. Take it for a test drive and you'll see exactly what I mean.

For example: You are in very good company if you are not feeling a strong connection with your baby… *yet*.

Here's another way to think about it: some believe in love at first sight (i.e., an instant connection), while others have found it takes time to build a strong bond. Both statements can be true without diminishing the other. No matter what you believe, the final outcome is the same: *connection* — regardless of how long it takes you to get there.

BIOLOGY

Let's face it, as men, biology isn't exactly on our side when it comes to nurturing a substantial connection with our little ones — especially prior to birth. According to a study published in the Journal of Obstetric, Gynecologic, & Neonatal Nursing (JOGNN), "fathers reported that they didn't start to experience fatherhood until [after the] birth [of their child]," while moms reported that they started to experience motherhood as soon as they received news that they were pregnant.[1] This isn't extremely shocking, but it does mean that men often find themselves a bit behind in the bonding department. For many of us, until we see our child for the first time, it can be quite difficult to truly grasp the realities of fatherhood.

Without a baby growing in our belly, it simply does not always feel real. I have no doubt that during the nine(ish) months your baby grew outside of your body, there were moments you forgot about the major life change coming your way. Maybe you were lost in something with work or on your phone. It's completely understandable. I certainly forgot from time to time.

We don't experience any physical reminders kicking us at random hours to say, "Hey, I'm still here and on my way!"

It makes sense that the baby might not feel real until we first see them or hold them in our arms. Therefore, it's not surprising that some might feel a bit shell-shocked when this hypothetical becomes a reality — and can no longer be ignored or forgotten (even if accidentally).

And again, all of this might not be the case for you. You may experience love at first sight. But if you don't, know that it's relatively common to not feel anything at all. And it doesn't mean there's something wrong with you.

It even goes beyond biology. Researchers at Oxford University studied fifteen fathers over an eight-month period (beginning just before their children were born), and observed that regardless of their intentions about sharing roles with their partners, "found they were ending up in quite traditional structures where mother raised the child and father worked to support them."[2] Anna Machin, the evolutionary anthropologist conducting the research, added "that the attitude of wider society relegated them to the role of supporter rather than parent."[3]

But that simply means that we, as dads, must remember the importance of being our own advocates. We have to be willing to chart our own path.

When it came to parenting, I was determined to break traditional gender norms, but in the beginning, I still found myself feeling like an outsider — disconnected from both my baby and my co-parent. Like many new moms, my wife got so infatuated with our new baby that she not only forgot I existed, but also unknowingly failed to recognize that I might want some time with our baby as well.

And I'm not alone in this — I've interviewed countless new dads with similar experiences. As mentioned in Myth #2, at least two-thirds of new dads are said to admit to feeling left out in the early days of parenting.[4]

But this doesn't have to be the case. Want to know how I handled it?

I Refused to Give Up!

"Whatever edge a mother may have hormonally or biologically, all three parties have to begin forming relationships at birth," says Michael Lamb, Ph.D., developmental psychologist and a leading authority on the role of fathers in child development. "The more time you spend with a child and the more things you do with them, the quicker the relationship develops and the stronger it becomes — regardless of the parent's sex."[5]

In short, don't wait for an invitation. Just dive in.

One of the easiest ways to bond is with something called skin-to-skin contact* (SSC), a simple action where you snuggle your newborn on your bare chest. This allows your baby to hear your heartbeat and learn your smell, just as they do with a mom if breastfeeding. Similar to all of the actions detailed in Myth #1, this is as much for your newborn as it is for you!

> **Simple SSC Exercise**
> Try laying your baby, in just their diaper, on your bare chest. Make sure to support their head with it tilted to the side so they can breathe. Cover their back with a blanket to keep them warm. Then just relax together for around an hour (or more if able).

SSC between father and child, done as soon as possible after birth, has been proven to positively enhance connection.[6] And this applies to any dad — no matter how you came to fatherhood, including dads through surrogacy or adoption who can practice SSC at their first meeting — whether in the hospital, agency, or at home. Regular uninterrupted SSC is a way to jump-start that bonding process for those of us that did not carry our baby for almost a year of our lives. It can also be a reminder of how capable we modern dads can actually be.

MYTH #3 — YOU WILL FEEL AN INSTANT BOND WITH YOUR BABY

For me, SSC was a life-saver in every sense of the term. Our birth story was a complicated one. I don't bring this up to scare you if you have not yet welcomed your child into the world — everything worked out beautifully in the end — but it wasn't all butterflies and rainbows. My wife had a high-risk pregnancy with a very difficult birth. Our baby was quickly taken to the NICU (neonatal intensive care unit), and my wife was rushed off to emergency surgery. I was terrified and in no way felt any connection to my newborn son.

While in the NICU, I noticed that my son would not stop crying. It was hard for anyone not to notice. He was also covered in tubes. At a bit of a loss, I gathered up all my courage and asked the nearest nurse if I could pick my baby up and do some SSC. I thought maybe I could help to calm him.

The nurse laughed in my face.

I then (as politely as I could) insisted that she hand me my baby.

I took off my shirt as they removed whatever tubes they could, and I put my son on my bare chest. I'd read that SSC could be a powerful bonding mechanism, but I never expected what happened next.

Almost instantaneously, he stopped crying.

The thought of that experience still brings tears to my eyes — both the trauma of it and the joy. That moment was the first time I felt connected to my son… and my new role as his dad. It was also the first time I understood the importance of being my own dadvocate.

Whereas women's levels of oxytocin — a natural hormone released in the brain, promoting feelings of love and attachment — surge during pregnancy and birth to facilitate bonding, studies suggest that oxytocin levels only truly surge for fathers through physical time spent caring for their children.[7] That could mean anything from SSC to singing, talking or simply reading to your newborn (all of which help with early brain and language development).[8] It could also mean taking the lead on diaper changes, rocking your little one to the *Point of Calm* (we'll delve more into this when we get to Myth #5), or simply making the effort to Co-Feed.

Remember that study I mentioned earlier that revealed many fathers only felt they became a *true* parent after sharing feeding responsibilities? Believe it. The more actively involved you are early on, the more connected you will feel to your baby.

And it goes both ways. Bonding between father and child during the fourth trimester has also been shown to have several benefits for your baby: it reduces cognitive delay, promotes weight gain in preterm infants, promotes healthy brain development, and even improves breastfeeding rates.[9]

"Father-infant bonding is an issue that is not discussed enough and is just as important as mother-infant bonding during the immediate postpartum* period," said Lynn Erdman, Chief Executive Officer of the Association of Women's Health, Obstetric and Neonatal Nurses (AWHONN). "It is vitally important for a father to interact and bond with his newborn to help the infant's development."[10] It's also an important factor in reducing the risk of many mental health struggles like heightened anxiety and depression that can affect new parents, regardless of their gender.

The key word here is "interact." As with any relationship, you can't expect a strong bond to form if you are not putting in the time. Every one of these positive interactions has the potential to show your baby that you are ready and available — not only to acknowledge, but also accommodate their needs. It's also one of the first steps in establishing something known as a secure attachment*, which is when a caregiver (whether biologically-related or not) is consistently responsive, sensitive, and emotionally available to their child's needs. This is a bond that is said to be crucial for healthy social and emotional development.[11] It's also one of the best ways to form a strong connection with anyone, no matter who they are.

The first step is simple: carve out some dedicated one-on-one time with your little one. As previously mentioned, I asked to take ownership of the night shift around one month in. I found that time alone with my baby brought about some of my most memorable moments as a new parent, where I first saw a glimpse of my connection with my future bestie.

CHOICES

I once heard a theory that if feeling left out on the home front, dads often take one of three paths. Some, unfortunately, run away. Some stay but disengage, going into their own heads (potentially) as a form of self-preservation. Others attempt to gain attention through comedy (or at least attempts at it) — which might be the true origin behind the term "Dad Joke."

However, I believe there's one more path — a stronger choice for all involved:

Engage MORE

Although I did feel a strong connection with my son in the NICU, the trauma of the whole experience still took its toll. During the first few weeks, I often found myself giving up when I could not quickly stop his crying, and I believe my son felt it. Kids are extremely empathetic — especially babies. They're sponges! They aren't lost in their heads. They have no walls built up from a life of emotional shrapnel being thrown their way. They are 100% present and available. Therefore, *your* energy can greatly affect *their* mood. So, if you're uncomfortable, there's a good chance your little one feels your hesitation.

In my situation, it's like my son knew that I was on the verge of giving up. I now know that this energy was partly due to other factors we'll touch on in the next chapter, but even without that knowledge, something from within told me I had to show my son — and myself — that I was not going anywhere.

I remember when he was around six weeks old. I had been handling the night shift for a bit, so I had already done a number of night feeds. By this point I was more comfortable with him, but any connection I felt was a bit one sided as he was usually half asleep during the feeds.

This time was different though. It was around 3 a.m. My wife was passed out, and my son was *very* unhappy. If he could speak, I'm sure he would have said, "Get my Mommy NOWWWW!!!"

In this scenario, many would have simply woken their co-parent, but I knew my wife needed her rest. Whether it was pride or a deep desire for a stronger connection, I refused to give up.

I already felt like my son preferred his mom — after all, she had carried him and supplied him with all the necessities to enter this world. Up to this point, she had also mostly been his sole food source. Although I knew it was not a competition (at least that's what I tried to tell myself), the truth is that I was beginning to get a bit resentful of her connection with our child. But I also knew their bond did not mean that we could not have a strong bond as well — and I repeated that to myself silently on a regular basis.

But I digress. Back to that fateful night. I rocked my wailing baby on a bouncy ball for an hour as he screamed in my ear. It was rough. I was honestly a bit beside myself, but I was committed to owning the task at hand. I simply repeated the words "you are safe" about a hundred times (to both my son and myself) and then, out of nowhere, he stopped crying. He relaxed. He gave in.

And in that moment, it all clicked. It was like he was testing me. He wanted to confirm that I was in it for the long haul, and I had passed the test. I'd survived the battle, and we were both stronger for it. It never again took anywhere near as long for me to calm him and to this day, the words "you are safe" still have a calming impact. But in every fiber of my being, I know that it wasn't about the words I chose or how long it took — it was about him knowing that I was there, and I was not going anywhere.

FOCUS

Aside from putting in the time and refusing to give up, there is one additional piece of the puzzle that is crucial to forming a long-lasting connection with your partner, child, or anyone for that matter — *focus*.

To actually bond with another person in a way that truly benefits all parties involved — including you — you'll need to avoid multitasking and devote your full attention to the person you are engaging with. I know that in today's "always-on" world, this is not an easy thing to ask, but it will make all the difference. Focus is the key element to fully engaging in any activity, but especially when it comes to building strong connections.

Imagine you're on a date with a potential partner who you just might want to spend the rest of your life with. What do you think would happen if you spent the entire evening scrolling social media while responding to texts and emails? You think you'd really have the ability to get to know one another? That they would feel comfortable enough with you to let down their guard? Do you think they would ever want to see you again?

Most of the time, dates to remember are the ones where

you allow yourself to get swept away. Where you make an effort to remove all distractions in order to focus all your attention on your date. Well, this same theory applies to building any connection with another individual, romantic or not — including your kid.

Every dad I've ever interviewed has agreed: you can't multitask a strong relationship with your child. And let's face it, many new dads (with partners who gave birth) often feel like the second choice. We didn't give birth to the kid, we don't have boobs that can potentially feed and console our babies. So we have to be creative. And creativity demands focus.

So, consider keeping your phone in the other room during bonding time. Or better yet, turn it off!

If you want to bond with your kid in a way that makes them feel safe and connected to you — while simultaneously putting a smile on your face when reminiscing about your time together — you will need to make every effort to eliminate any and all distractions.

Once you lay that foundation of dedicated focus, there are innumerable actions you can take on a daily basis to strengthen your bond with your baby:

- Rock them while you tell them a story

- Sing to them while walking around the house or even just sitting on the couch

- Read them a book (in these early months, it's less about what you read and more about the act itself)

- Put them in a carrier or stroller and go for a walk while telling them about your day — it's not the topic that's important, but the talking, and your baby getting familiar with your voice

But no matter what actions you choose, don't underestimate the power of eye contact. It may sound silly with an infant, but think about how different it feels when you share a conversation with a friend, co-worker or even your co-parent using eye contact versus without. Consistent eye contact provides a safer, more vulnerable environment — more aligned with building a strong connection (which is the point of all of this, no?).

With regular eye contact, your baby should soon begin to recognize you while associating your facial features with the way they feel when you are together — which means you'll both be well on your way to an enduring connection that will last a lifetime.

IN CLOSING

Concerns about forming an instant bond with your child are extremely common amongst both expectant and new parents. The first line of defense is expressing your concerns with others. Please know that if a bond does not form immediately, there is *nothing* wrong with you — it can take time.

If you feel left out when your baby first arrives home, talk with your co-parent. If months have passed and you're still worried that you haven't bonded with your baby, talk to your pediatrician. They can help determine whether a greater issue may be at play.

But most importantly: DON'T GIVE UP!

Be patient. Be present. Put in the dedicated time, and the reward will be felt for years to come.

MYTH #4

POSTPARTUM DEPRESSION IS NOT A REAL THING

Many new moms experience something known as "baby blues," which is often associated with hormone drops after childbirth and can include everything from anxiety and insomnia to mood swings and crying spells.[1] Baby blues usually begin within the first two to three days after delivery and, in some cases, could last for up to two weeks. However, if those feelings don't subside after two weeks — or worsen with feelings of emptiness, sadness, or hopelessness — your co-parent may have postpartum depression* (PPD).[2] This is a very real medical condition, and anyone experiencing PPD should be encouraged to seek out professional assistance by reaching out to their OB or a licensed healthcare professional.

PMADs

Unfortunately, there is a long list of misconceptions surrounding PPD[3], but I believe one of the most overlooked is the fact that PPD is actually part of a larger umbrella of mental health struggles called perinatal mood and anxiety disorders* or PMADs.[4] Although not yet a popularized term, PMADs are more common than one might think and can actually be experienced by *any* new parent, including moms through surrogacy or adoption and dads[5] of every shape and form. In fact, mental health struggles in new dads are quite common, but far less frequently diagnosed.[6]

Think about it: how many times did anyone ask you how you were feeling after first announcing you were going to become a dad — while genuinely giving you the space to answer honestly? How about throughout the pregnancy? Or during the fourth trimester? Truth be told, I didn't even think to ask myself!

Now, you might be thinking, why would anyone ask me? As men, we're trained, and with good reason, to focus all our attention on our pregnant partners. It almost feels selfish to think about our own needs. We're not the ones carrying the baby. I saw how my wife was struggling. How could I think about myself?

However, I now know that as crucial as it is for new parents to find ways to support their co-parent, it is just as crucial to take care of yourself.

Becoming a parent is a huge life change — for *all* involved. Allowing yourself the space to feel whatever you might be feeling will not inherently take anything away from what others may be experiencing — particularly when it comes to past fertility struggles or miscarriage. Those kinds of struggles don't just magically disappear when a new baby arrives.

Acknowledging my feelings (even just to myself) probably would have been extremely beneficial to both me and my partner. That being said, I am well aware that people rarely like to admit when they're struggling. It often feels easier to simply downplay any difficulties since almost every new parent deals with a certain amount of anxiety and exhaustion with a newborn. However, if those struggles become excessive and difficult to manage, interfering with day-to-day activities, it may be a sign of a larger mental health issue.

Mental health struggles arising after the birth of your child can occur due to a wide array of potential risk factors. The most commonly discussed for PMADs is hormonal changes, which are most often associated with women post birth.

Less commonly known is that fathers can *also* experience hormonal changes when becoming a new dad — particularly declines in testosterone.[7]

There's even evidence that men's brains transform after the arrival of a new baby. Lee Gettler, who co-authored a study on the topic, said, "Fatherhood and the demands of having a newborn baby require many emotional, psychological and physical adjustments. Our study indicates that a man's biology can change substantially to help meet those demands."[8] In short, not only do our hearts metaphorically grow, our brain literally changes.

Also less commonly known is that there are a number of *other* potential risk factors that could trigger mental health issues for new parents — regardless of gender, sexual orientation or biological relation to your child[9] — including but not limited to:

- Sleep deprivation
- Change of identity
- Change in relationship dynamics
- Lack of support
- A co-parent struggling with PPD
- Pre-existing factors, such as family history or past struggles (e.g., infertility, depression, past loss)

Of the six risk factors listed above, I personally experienced five:

1. **Sleep Deprivation (√)**

   Obviously, any actively-involved parent will likely experience a lack of sleep with a newborn, but most new parents underestimate how much that lack of sleep can assist in developing symptoms of anxiety and depression — we'll dive more into how to tackle this in Myth #5.

2. **Change of Identity (√)**

   The psychological adjustment and weight of responsibility (not to mention the added financial pressures) that accompany the newly crowned title of parent can be overwhelming, regardless of gender — this one is hard to avoid. It honestly just takes time.

3. **Change in Relationship Dynamics (√)**

   For me, the change in relationship dynamics came from feeling disconnected from my partner-in-crime, who previously was a huge part of my support system. Justifiably, she now had a new primary focus, but that often left me feeling invisible. She was obviously not intentionally leaving me out, but that didn't make the rejection hurt any less. We'll dive more into this in Myth #7.

4. **Lack of Support (√)**

   As a new dad, I personally felt a gaping hole of available resources that otherwise seemed readily available to almost every new mom I encountered. As mentioned, that was one of the main inspirations for the launch of my podcast, which quickly evolved into a platform to better support dads by sharing their stories — reminding each and every one of us that we are rarely alone in any of the struggles we may be experiencing.

5. **Pre-Existing Factors (√)**

   This was a big one for me. My wife and I struggled to get pregnant for five years. During that time period, I tried throwing myself into work, but often struggled to find the passion that had made my work fulfilling in the past. I attempted to pack our social calendar to the point of exhaustion. I put on a smile as I watched our friends have their first babies, and for some, second and third. But behind closed doors, I was falling into a deep depression. The experience nearly tore our marriage apart.

MYTH #4 – POSTPARTUM DEPRESSION IS NOT A REAL THING

Not only are men often trained from an early age to push down our feelings, but every conversation with others during our fertility struggles was focused on my wife. Therefore, it felt completely justified that she should be our sole focus during that strenuous time period. But if I knew that simply taking the time to acknowledge my feelings aloud would have immensely helped in the healing process, I would have done it a lot sooner.

Once we finally learned we were expecting, we were ecstatic. And yet, all that pain and suffering from years of trying was still there. I didn't want it to be. It wasn't a choice. I think some part of me knew I was not okay, but hoped that any struggles I was experiencing would simply evaporate with time. But that's when I learned one of the most difficult lessons of my life to date: Ignored feelings eventually bubble back up, stronger than ever before, and ultimately help no one — least of all our families, who need us at our best for the journey ahead.

With all the risk factors listed above, by the time I hit one month in as a parent, I no longer recognized myself in the mirror — I am living proof that men can experience PMADs.

The Research

Although there's historically been little discussion surrounding paternal mental health, there has been an increase of coverage within the past few years, including an eye-opening essay in *The New York Times* called "I Gave Birth, but My Husband Developed Postpartum Depression."[10]

One of the few studies on this topic found that at least 1 in 10 new dads experience mental health struggles following the birth of their baby.[11] However, many cases go unreported and that number could actually climb as high as 25%,[12] especially within the first 3-6 months following the birth of their child — in other words, impacting 1 in 4 new dads!

"That's more than twice the rate of depression we usually see in men," explains James F. Paulson, Ph.D., lead author of a survey assessing 43 studies on depression in new fathers of more than 28,000 men worldwide. "The fact that so many expecting and new dads go through it makes it a significant public-health concern — one that physicians and mental-health providers have largely overlooked."[13]

According to Sheehan D. Fisher, a perinatal clinical psychologist at Northwestern University, symptoms of perinatal mental health issues can differ between men and women, which may be one of the reasons many men go undiagnosed — as well as a lack of awareness that the diagnosis even exists.[14]

Although there is much less research on the topic, PMAD symptoms[15] in men may include:

- Uncharacteristic irritability or anger
- Feelings of hopelessness
- Obsessive or compulsive behavior
- Panic attacks
- Desire for constant isolation
- An increase in dopamine-boosting activities (e.g., alcohol/substance abuse)
- Hypersexuality
- Insomnia
- Thoughts of self-harm

The Good News

The good news is that PMADs do not have to take over your life, and can be treated with varying combinations of self-care*, social support, talk therapy, and, if needed, medication.[16] If you are experiencing any of the symptoms detailed above or have concerns, please consider reaching out to a licensed healthcare professional — you truly have nothing to lose and everything to gain.

What is Self-Care?

Self-care refers to the proactive steps one can take to maintain and improve their physical, mental, and emotional well-being. Methods can vary based on personal preference, but could include anything from meditation, cooking or working out to simply taking some alone time to do an activity that calms you — from journaling to chopping wood. So find yourself an axe or check out more mind-calming options in Myth #9.

"Men need to recognize that depression [and any other mental health issue that arises after the birth of your child] is a medical condition; it's not a weakness of character," says Dr. Will Courtenay, PhD, LCSW, and a psychotherapist focused on men's health. "For a man to admit he's depressed isn't unmanly or admitting defeat. It's taking charge of his life."[17]

To be clear, PMADs are not something that everyone experiences, but if you do notice that something is off, try to remember that no good will come from letting ego or pride prevent you from asking for help. Again, you do not need permission to feel whatever it is you may be feeling. How can you be expected to best support your partner or family if you're falling apart on the inside?

If you still don't believe that your feelings (whatever they may be) are just as valid as every other parent on the planet, also know that when *either* parent experiences any form of a mental health struggle, it can affect how they care for and bond with their baby — which can ultimately impact their child's social, intellectual, and emotional development.[18]

The motivation behind this chapter is not to instill fear, but rather to raise awareness, especially for those who view the concept of paternal mental health struggles as complete fiction. The truth is that each of the potential risk factors previously mentioned are much more common for new dads than most realize.

Regardless if you are struggling with any signs of PMADs, I cannot express enough the significance of taking the time to communicate whatever it is you are feeling, including any fears or anxieties. And yes, this may require you to drop any protective armor that has been built up through the years, as well as the facade that we as men don't have any feelings or vulnerabilities to share. Bottled up feelings have a way of intensifying — often resulting in some form of internal combustion. And the aftermath can hurt those we care for in critical ways that could have been avoided had we simply dropped our guard and let them in.

As discussed in Myth #1, one of the easiest ways to seek assistance is by turning to your support system. If you don't feel like you have one (and trust me, you're in good company), it's never too late to begin forming one. There's a reason they say, *it takes a village*. It's not just about getting assistance in raising your kid, it's also about staying sane while doing it.

Proof Relationships Matter

If you're still not convinced about the importance of a strong support network, consider this: in an ever-expanding study over nearly 80 years (one of the world's longest analyses of adult life), the Harvard Study of Adult Development tracked the health of hundreds of men (including future President John F. Kennedy), as well as a number of their offspring. The study revealed that close relationships, when nurtured — more than any other factor, including career or money — are what provide people with the most contentment throughout their lives.[19]

"Taking care of your body is important, but tending

to your relationships is a form of self-care too," said Robert Waldinger, director of the study and a professor of psychiatry at Harvard Medical School. "When we gathered together everything we knew about them at age 50, it wasn't their middle-age cholesterol levels that predicted how they were going to grow old. It was how satisfied they were in their relationships. The people who were the most satisfied in their relationships at age 50 were the healthiest at age 80."[20]

The two biggest gifts you can offer yourself are the space to adjust to this new normal, and the courage to seek out support when needed.

IN CLOSING

The first year of becoming a new parent (regardless of gender) can be filled with intoxicating joy, but it can also be quite difficult. Hiding any feelings or concerns benefits NO ONE and will only inevitably do more damage than good for the whole family.

The best thing you can do for yourself and your loved ones is take the time to acknowledge whatever it is you are feeling, and then openly discuss those feelings with others. If there's one thing that I can guarantee, it's that whatever you are feeling, you are *not* alone.

MYTH #5

YOU WILL NEVER SLEEP AGAIN

This is total malarkey. However, the *amount* of sleep you get will honestly depend on a variety of factors. Some will be completely out of your control, but many can be influenced by the systems and strategies you put into place.

Although getting some solid rest with a newborn can be a challenge, there are a number of things you can do to sway the odds in your favor. The following is a short list of recommendations, but of course, the final decision on what to implement will come down to whatever makes the most sense for your family, based upon the intricacies of your life.

STRATEGY 1:
FREEDOM SHIFTS

If you happen to have a co-parent on this wild ride we call parenthood, why not take full advantage of each other's support? Teamwork is one of the most effective ways to not only get some much-needed rest, but also build in some time to recharge your battery! Even beyond the newborn stage, I strongly encourage all parents to implement a system I like to call: *Freedom Shifts[1]*.

In short, when one co-parent is on duty (for a previously agreed-upon time period), the other is *free* to do as they see fit — in other words, take a Freedom Shift* — without any responsibility whatsoever.

For many new parents, the first inclination is to use their Freedom Shift to catch up on sleep — which is completely understandable. Unfortunately, too often, a Freedom Shift can be wasted in a stressed-out state, replaying your list of "shoulds" and to-dos. And who can fall asleep when their mind is racing?

In order to get some shut eye (and actually clear your mind), it's important to step away and take some time for yourself. One of the most important aspects of a Freedom Shift is the opportunity to refocus your attention back onto *your* needs, because even as a parent, you are still someone who deserves that right.

Remembering that you are a human being with needs of your own can often help to release the pressure gauge and let go of any pent-up frustrations. Once you become a parent, much of your time and focus becomes about the needs of your child or your family. However, a Freedom Shift is a time to think about what *you* may need, without any guilt or concern that you are letting anyone else down.

To be clear, Freedom Shifts are not a time to catch up on work (that time should be allotted elsewhere), but rather a time for calming activities for your mind, body and soul — from a workout to reading a good book to catching up with an old friend — that is, if and when you have the energy to do so.

Returning from a Freedom Shift refreshed and rejuvenated is the best gift you can offer to your family, and will likely help in future interactions with both your baby and your co-parent. Of course, this system *only* works if you allot a similar amount of time for your co-parent to take their own Freedom Shifts.

It should be noted that this system requires the person holding down the fort (the one *not* on their Freedom Shift) to be essentially "on call" during their agreed-upon hours. If you are the one on duty, and the baby sleeps through much of the night, you can use the time as you wish — hanging out with your co-parent or getting some rest. However, anything the baby needs during that time period (from calming to feeding to diaper changes) is on you. Meanwhile, the co-parent on their Freedom Shift should feel free to go for a walk, put in some ear plugs and take a bath, or get some much-needed sleep, guilt-free.

The choice of how to divide up shifts is completely up to you and your co-parent. I am not implying that you should divide up the entirety of your time and never allow for any family bonding. However, there will be times when you each simply need a break from responsibility.

If you are a night-owl, you could cover the night shift from bedtime duties to dream feeds* while your co-parent takes a Freedom Shift. If you are a morning person, why not give your co-parent the chance to sleep in or go for a guilt-free jog while you take control of morning duties. If neither of you has a preference, simply pick one and keep to it — but if you share the same preference, one of you will need to suck it up.

And for those who feel their work schedule impedes their ability to handle either morning or night duties, you might try covering dinnertime or bedtime (or both), so your co-parent has at least a few hours to rest — both mind and body — while also allowing you some crucial time to bond with your little one.

The Importance of Assigning Shifts

I once had a stay-at-home dad (SAHD) tell me that he and his husband were planning to simply "share" all responsibilities regarding their baby as opposed to specifically assigning any shifts. But before long, he reached out to complain that he had covered all the night feeds for the past three weeks as well as handling mornings. He assumed his co-parent would get the hint after countless subtle drops about how exhausted he was. He even went so far as to stay in bed and pretend to be sleeping when the baby began screaming at 3 a.m. — like a stand-off between two people at a restaurant avoiding the check while waiting for the other to make a move. Eventually, SAHD jumped up after his co-parent screamed his name. Clearly, this situation was not working.

SAHD admitted to feeling guilty because he had agreed to be the one to stay home and care for their newborn while his husband went to work, but he was feeling burnt out and needed more support. Resentments were building and he found himself constantly snapping at his co-parent. After some encouragement, SAHD voiced his concerns. His co-parent confessed that he felt the tension, but was oblivious as to how exhausted SAHD actually was. SAHD's co-parent also confessed that he had not been sleeping well either. He felt guilty about not handling more around the house, but with his early morning work meetings, he honestly felt exhausted as well. Most importantly though, he admitted to feeling a bit disconnected from the baby, and was insecure about his ability to successfully handle any night feeds.

They both agreed that assigning some shifts could help in multiple ways, particularly in eliminating any gray areas around who was responsible for what. As his hectic work schedule was not allowing for much morning or daytime bonding, SAHD's co-parent agreed to handle bedtime every night but Thursdays when he took his own Freedom Shift from both work and home responsibilities. SAHD would keep handling the dream feeds every evening but Fridays, when his co-parent would handle the entire night shift from bedtime to morning — giving SAHD a Freedom Shift. SAHD would also continue handling mornings every day except Sundays, when his co-parent would take over, allowing SAHD to sleep in and get some much-needed rest before the start of the new week.

MYTH #5 – YOU WILL NEVER SLEEP AGAIN

Again, like everything in this book, the specifics of the systems you put in place are up to you. I am more of a night owl with a more flexible morning work schedule. Therefore, during our parental leave, I covered from bedtime at 7 p.m. to 5 a.m., while my co-parent took their Freedom Shift, caught up on sleep, and then handled 5 a.m. to 12 p.m. Yes, my time on-the-clock was a bit longer, but our baby was more likely to sleep during my time slot.

Now, there will be some who will struggle with the concept of Freedom Shifts. Those who have trouble relinquishing control may have difficulty *not* jumping up when they hear their baby crying — even when on their Freedom Shift. This is understandable; however, for this system to work (and for each co-parent to rediscover some sanity in their day-to-day lives), that individual needs to try their best to trust that their co-parent has it handled.

In our relationship, I was the one with the difficulty and I quickly learned that if parents do not fully and consistently utilize their Freedom Shifts, this system *will* fail. Therefore, even if I was awoken in the morning (during my Freedom Shift), I did my darnedest to trust that my co-parent had it handled… or would eventually figure it out. My sole job was to breathe and attempt to give my body (and mind) some needed relaxation.

At a minimum, know that allotting the time for at least one Freedom Shift per week to do whatever the heck you want — with no oversight and no judgment — can leave you feeling refreshed and better prepared to take on whatever gets thrown your way.

STRATEGY 2:
BE THE CALM IN THE EYE OF THE STORM

Obviously, the easiest way to get any sleep with a newborn is to get your newborn to sleep. Although this can sometimes feel like a daunting task, one of the best places to start is actually with *you*.

Studies show that even infants are affected by their parent's mood. "From birth, infants pick up on emotional cues from others. Even very young infants look to caregivers to determine how to react to a given situation," says Jennifer E. Lansford, PhD, a professor with the Social Science Research Institute and the Center for Child and Family Policy at Duke University.[2]

In short, kids are sponges, so *your* energy is extremely important to consider. It's quite impractical to think you can calm a baby when you are not calm. The more gentle your energy, the more relaxed your baby will often become (which is what makes the need for Freedom Shifts — and taking the time to reset — all the more important). Your little one may not follow your lead immediately, but give it a beat. Almost all humans require a cool-down period after a long day to transition the mind and body to a more restful state — shouldn't babies be given that same courtesy?

Now comes the inevitable question of *how* to remain calm. True, the first few months as a new parent can be quite stressful and overwhelming at times — even after implementing the Freedom Shift system. However, there is one universal theory that can help when encountering stressful situations involving another person:

> *We can rarely control what another individual says, does or feels.*
>
> *The only thing we have complete control over is how we respond.*[3]

Notice that the word "respond" is purposefully used instead of "react."

Whereas reacting to any given situation is purely emotional without any thought of the consequences, responding takes into consideration a specific desired outcome. In order to attempt to ensure a positive outcome, it's crucial to take a moment *before* we respond to any situation — a moment to take back ownership of our own emotions.

Truth be told, this concept applies to interactions with any human on the planet (no matter their age). However, let's apply it to a crying baby — often one of the biggest obstacles to any rest within the first few months of becoming a parent.

MYTH #5 – YOU WILL NEVER SLEEP AGAIN

Ever tried to get a task done with someone sitting over you screaming, "Are you done yet?" I think we can all agree that it makes it harder to complete the task at hand. And that becomes exponentially more true when it comes to calming another person.

Getting stressed out or intensely shushing for your baby to relax will unlikely have the desired effect. It's actually quite absurd to think we can stop a baby from crying. The best we can do is attempt to create a safe and calming atmosphere for the baby to *choose* — even subconsciously — to stop crying.

Obviously, the practice of patience is key here, although not always our go-to as humans. One of the best techniques available is not only free, but one you are most likely already quite familiar with:

Deep breaths

The benefits will be apparent the moment you take advantage of this simple action — alright, it might take more than a moment, but give it a chance!

When stressed, the brain prioritizes sending oxygen to muscles as part of our body's fight-or-flight response — often neglecting the prefrontal cortex (the area responsible for rational thinking).[4] Therefore, a few deep breaths can help deliver oxygen to this area, allowing for calmer reactions to the situation at hand.

Breathing Exercise

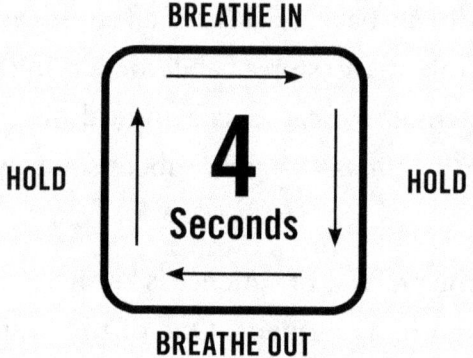

The 4x4 breathing technique — also known as box breathing* — is a controlled breathing exercise, renowned for its effectiveness in managing stress and anxiety.[5] By distracting your mind as you count to four, this exercise (favored by US Navy SEALs in high stress situations) can help you slow down your breathing, while calming your nervous system and decreasing stress in your body.

Focus on breathing deeply from your abdomen through your nose, filling the lungs slowly and steadily while counting to four prior to exhaling.

Breathe in through nose for count of 4, hold for 4, exhale through mouth for count of 4, hold for 4, and repeat 4 times.

Esther Sternberg, a physician and researcher at the National Institute of Mental Health insists that deep breaths can be used as a method to train the body's reaction to stressful situations. They can also dampen the production of harmful stress hormones.[6] Maybe that's why it's often said that deep breaths are like little love notes to your body and mind (awww).

And this same strategy applies when interacting with your co-parent. Losing your cool with each other will rarely help the situation. One of the benefits to having a co-parent is that you can balance one another out. Everyone has bad days. Sometimes you might lose your cool (which happens to everyone!), but hopefully your co-parent can have your back and talk you off the ledge — and then you can do the same for them when they're in need.

Allowing the time for a few deep breaths when encountering a stressful situation is truly one of the simplest paths to a less chaotic existence — although, admittedly, easier in theory than in practice. Patience will get you everywhere in life, and although any solutions may not come to you immediately, you surely won't find them without a clear mind. It can also help in forming new habits to control how we respond to the chaos.

In summary, if you want to take advantage of any opportunities for sleep that may present themselves (as well as for the benefit of your relationship with your baby, your co-parent, or your own personal well-being), try to stay calm. The next time you get stressed, try taking a few deep breaths *before* you react — allowing yourself the space to best formulate how to respond in order to achieve the most ideal outcome. The added benefit of mastering this strategy is that it will not only help prepare your baby for sleep, but also calm them (and yourself) no matter what obstacles may arise.

STRATEGY 3:
THE EMPATHIC METHOD

Yes, the first three months can be a rollercoaster for new parents — there's no denying it. And although it definitely starts to normalize a bit once you get through the fourth trimester, it can be extremely difficult to get any rest with a crying baby in the house (or while you are steaming in frustration). Aside from Freedom Shifts and deep breaths, another great strategy to keeping a level head (and again, more able to take advantage of the opportunity for sleep when it presents itself) is to allow yourself to see things from a different perspective — particularly your baby's.

One of the greatest things I've learned thus far from working within the parenting space (and something that will save you much frustration and strained relations down the line) is the simple concept that once your baby enters your home, there is now an additional human being present. I know this may seem obvious or even silly to some, but I can't tell you the amount of parents that forget that from day one, this little being is slowly formulating their own feelings and preferences.

This means that just because you're tired or have work to do, does not mean that they want to sleep. And the harder you force the issue, the harder they will likely resist. So, why not try thinking about things from *their* perspective?

Imagine if all you knew was floating around, safe and snug in a dark cave with muffled sounds (i.e., the womb), and then all of a sudden (without your permission), you were thrust into an unpredictable world of bright lights, loud noises, and flailing appendages you didn't even fully realize were attached to your body. Is it not understandable that you would be a bit overwhelmed?! And would you not cry and scream a good amount as well?

Think about it: if your baby seems upset and it feels bright to you, it's probably much brighter for the person who has basically lived in darkness for the past nine months. If the baby seems upset and hasn't been rocked in quite some time — remember that their "normal" has been shuffling around in the womb for as long as they can remember (while the person who carried them walked around and lived their life). If the baby is upset and the room is very quiet — remember that your baby has been listening to muffled sounds from the outside world since their inception and might appreciate some gentle music or calming sounds. I'm not saying these approaches will always work in calming your baby or getting them to sleep, but it's definitely a great place to start.

The ability to see things from another's perspective is one of the most important skills any parent can master. It will assist you greatly as your child grows and is introduced to the outside world. It also has the added benefit of getting you out of your own head — which can be an extremely isolating place to be during these first few (sometimes overwhelming) months.

Avoiding the Comparison Game

This has less to do directly with sleep, but will help you keep a level head when times get stressful — and bedtime can often be one of those times.

There is a strong chance that when speaking with other parents or when doing deep dives through social media or Google, you may find examples of children at a similar age to yours who appear to be advancing to the next developmental stage before your child. You might even hear stories of babies who seamlessly sleep through the night, which can be extremely frustrating for a parent who is living a very different reality.

However, comparing your baby to others and their developmental achievements (or *supposed* achievements, according to their parents) can be a dangerous game. It's understandable to feel concerned if your child ever seems developmentally behind, but it's always best to discuss your concerns with your child's pediatrician, rather than making up stories in your head.[7]

The fact is that playing the "comparison game" often plants expectations in your brain, which can add unnecessary pressure. This applies even when comparing your child to themselves and how long they slept a few nights back. Imagining how your night *could* look by playing the comparison game does not mean that's how it will turn out.

Expectations are a bit like poison. Reality will rarely match them, and you'll often be let down. Worse, they might blind you to the beautiful moments happening right before your eyes.

Every individual develops at their own pace, especially babies. I'm not saying it's abnormal to be aware of others (that would go against human nature), but the sooner you fight the urge to compare, the better off you'll be.

With this in mind, remember to never underestimate the power of the word *yet* — as in: the baby hasn't fallen asleep *yet*, the baby isn't rolling over *yet*, or the baby isn't sleeping through the night *yet*. Give it time.

ADDITIONAL TIPS

Although this book attempts to purposefully avoid dos and don'ts regarding your baby, I do have two sleep recommendations (based on dozens of interviews with new parents and sleep experts, as well as personal experience) that I believe will ultimately have a positive effect on your mental health as a parent — which is really what this book is all about. Take 'em or leave 'em:

Sleep Tactic 1:
Avoid Tiptoeing or Whispering While Your Baby Sleeps

This is pretty straight-forward. Try to avoid tiptoeing or sneaking around (or even whispering with your co-parent) once your kid falls asleep. I know you may be hesitant to wake a sleeping baby, but you might also be setting a precedent that you'll one day regret.

My wife took this tactic to heart when I first suggested it, and even went so far as to occasionally turn on the blender once our baby fell asleep — this may *sound* a bit extreme, but boy, did those smoothies taste like freedom.

For bonus points, when naptime or bedtime hits, rock and rub your little one to the Point of Calm*, but then attempt to lay them down *before* they fall asleep while removing yourself from their line of sight.

You don't necessarily need to leave their side. If you were singing to them, you can continue to do so as you put them down. But make sure they can no longer see you. If they fall asleep without your pretty face standing above them, they may be less shocked if they awake to find you no longer there (and more inclined to simply close their eyes and drift back off to sleep).

Of course, some nights will be easier than others, and everything goes out the window when your baby is sick — this is simply a mentality to strive for if you want to eventually work towards a more independent sleeper.

Again, every child is different, but I believe that at least avoiding any tiptoeing or whispering is worth a try, especially if you ever want to have friends over after your kid goes down or simply want to party it up with your co-parent.

Sleep Tactic 2:
Bedtime is Gentle Time

I know we've touched on this briefly, but when you begin your child's bedtime routine, I highly recommend putting away all devices in order to dedicate your full attention to your child. This is as much for your baby as it is for your own mental well-being.

At least 30 minutes prior to their bedtime (after bath and any other business of the night is done), dim the lights and try lowering the volume of your voice. I would even go so far as to recommend you slow the pace of your words. If you choose to read something, this may not be the best time to pull out your wildest and most exciting roster of impressions. Turn on some gentle music, soothing background sounds, or sing them a little Boyz II Men, and then allow for some calming cuddle time.

Mostly common sense, right?!

Here's where my advice may differ from others. If rocking your baby (working to get them to the Point of Calm before you lay them down), make sure you are both comfortable but not *too* comfortable. If you sit in a chair, you might both fall asleep, which means your baby may have a meltdown when awoken to you trying to leave. I recommend remaining in a standing position so the baby is comfortable, but not *so* comfortable that the bassinet or crib isn't a *more* comfortable option.

The Human Cradle

Another exercise I recommend is something I call *The Human Cradle** (inspired by my training in the Alexander Technique[8]): Basically, cradle your baby in your arms so none of their limbs are doing any work. For instance, their head is leaning either on your cheek with your hand on their opposite cheek (so their head is weightless) or resting on your shoulder (with their arms dangling).

In essence, their whole body is weightless, releasing any tension in the body. You'll find this technique can be of great assistance when attempting to relax a little one.

In summary, whether it's nap time or bedtime or even when putting a child back to sleep after they've woken up in the middle of the night, finding your way to an undistracted, gentle energy is essential for everyone involved, and could mean a better night's rest for the whole family.

IN CLOSING

The strategies provided in this chapter should not only assist in getting your baby to sleep, but also in bringing *you* some much-deserved calm. But as with everything on your parenting journey, I advise you to never take any advice so strictly that it goes against your gut.

Some of these strategies may not work for your family; however, if they do, don't be scared to make adjustments to make them your own. Any decisions you make on how you choose to raise your kid/s or put them to sleep are yours and yours alone.

Regardless of what techniques you choose, try to keep to one universal rule:

Be Consistent.

Consistency breeds a feeling of safety for every human on the planet (regardless of age), so that includes a baby where everything is new and already a bit chaotic. Consistency of routine can help a baby to anticipate what comes next, which can boost their confidence and help them to be more self-sufficient.[9] It's also just as important for a new parent, where things can feel a bit overwhelming at times. However, know that consistency does not mean rigidity — *some* flexibility within your ritual can get children comfortable with learning how to adapt without anxiety or stress. The point is to set up a consistent routine that you can be flexible within when needed.

As your baby adapts to a more stable sleep schedule (and you have a bit more energy), Freedom Shifts should move beyond an opportunity to simply catch up on sleep. But it is what it is during these first few months. However, that does not minimize the fact that sleep deprivation can be a very concerning issue, and can contribute to an array of serious chronic health problems[10] (including heart disease, high blood pressure, diabetes, obesity, and even PMADs); therefore, making the time to put some systems in place — whatever they may be — to help increase opportunities for sleep is well worth the effort.

MYTH #6

THERE'S NO ROOM FOR MISTAKES AS A PARENT

Here's the thing: we all say that it's okay to make mistakes, but that doesn't mean we like it when we do. Secretly, we're all terrified of making them — especially when it comes to our kids. Because we're scared our mistakes will F*#% them up.

Perhaps our focus would be better directed on how much room we allow ourselves (and those we love) to make mistakes... and then *learn* from them.

Like most parents trying to find their way, kids literally spend their entire adolescence (and beyond) attempting to find their footing in this big new world. How can they do that if they're terrified of making a mistake?

The best thing we can model is the acceptance that mistakes are inevitable, perhaps even necessary for any growth to occur. To take it one step further, Columbia University researchers found that when students make errors followed by corrective feedback, they learn better and ultimately remember the correct answers long-term.[1]

I know one parent who was so terrified of making a mistake that they were often paralyzed on the parenting front — like a robot awaiting future instruction. Not only does a situation like this tend to put all the weight on their co-parent's shoulders, it also rarely leads to a home filled with much joy. For any parent out there living in fear that making a mistake will ruin their child, it may be time to reframe your priorities.

ACCOUNTABILITY

The truth is that the mistakes are rarely what causes the damage, it's not being able to admit when you've made one. It's pretending to be perfect. It's brushing any missteps under the rug, and pretending they never happened. And one of the main reasons many do this is because they feel shame. In fact, one of the documented causes of shame is fearing your flaws or inadequacies will be revealed[2] — in other words, feeling the need to hide any imperfections or mistakes made. But torturing yourself and hiding any evidence that you are, indeed, human (and therefore *not* perfect) helps NO ONE.

One of my favorite books I've ever read with my kid (and I've read *a lot*[#]) is called *After The Fall (How Humpty Dumpty Got Back Up Again)*. After overcoming a fear of heights, Humpty makes his way back up to the top of the wall and rewrites the end of his story with the following inspirational sentiment:

> "Maybe now you won't think of me as that egg who was famous for falling. Hopefully, you'll remember me as the egg who got back up… and learned how to fly."[3]

> Use the QR code below to view DILF's list of kids books that parents will enjoy, too:
>
>

The true focus should not be on the mistakes, but rather on getting back up, forgiving ourselves, and learning from those mistakes. Because you'll make many — every parent does (whether they admit it or not). The only real damage comes from presenting a facade, ignoring your mistakes, and pretending you have it all figured out.

The best example we can be for our children (and our co-parent) is having the inner strength to not only acknowledge our missteps, but to own them with full accountability.

And by full accountability, I'm not talking about just apologizing for any mistake made — that's not nearly as important as vowing to not make that same mistake again. To flip the script. To learn from that mistake. And be better because of it.

TRANSPARENCY

Going a bit deeper though (and I know this may be a tough pill for some to swallow), full accountability is quite difficult to achieve without full transparency. If you make a mistake, and then *secretly* recognize that mistake, but attempt to sweep it under the rug and hope no one notices — well, that's not really being fully transparent. More importantly, you're missing an opportunity to show your kid that everyone makes mistakes and it's really no big deal.

Aside from verbally acknowledging any mistakes made to those affected by them (yes, even a baby), you might even try being transparent enough to clarify why you made that choice. It might even help you to discover a better future approach. Being fully transparent is often one of the clearest paths to seeing any error in our ways.

In full transparency, there have definitely been times that I've snapped at my kid without any legitimate justification. But as soon as I realize what I've done, I not only apologize but admit what is truly frustrating me (without going into *too* much detail). Maybe I'm stressed about work or I'm tired or don't feel good. Sure, I could simply justify my actions as no big deal, but I can guarantee you that the person being snapped at will not be so quick to forget.

Sometimes, transparently acknowledging an error in judgement aloud (and getting out of our heads) can remove the stigma from any given situation for all those involved. It can allow the mistake to simply float away into the ether, rather than be a topic your children discuss in therapy twenty years from now.

We all struggle at times, and it's important to be transparent about that fact. It also sets a precedent in our homes that life is a learning process, and making mistakes is a part of that — what better way to release the pressure valve that can often build up for kids (and even many adults).

And the same goes for any struggles that may arise with a co-parent.

I cannot tell you how many dads in my new-dad group have brought up concerns about getting into an argument with their co-parent in front of their baby. Either they try to avoid conflict at all costs and simply push down all frustrations — which never ends well. Or they got into it with their co-parent with their little one present, and are now concerned that they've traumatized their baby for life. It's a very common fear, but although conflict is never ideal, it's often unavoidable… and sometimes even necessary.

Parenting is stressful; especially life as a new parent. And although doing it with others can be a great asset, it's not always easy to consistently remain on the same page. Frustrations build. And disagreements can be a way to bring any of those unspoken (and sometimes unconscious) frustrations to light.

The real challenge is attempting to remain calm during any disagreements that may occur. Allowing everyone involved the chance to clear the air, and provide some perspective on where their heads are at. The trauma comes in when there are raised voices or name-calling (and of course, *any* violence), but having a transparent and respectful disagreement — even if it's in front of your child — is a whole different story.

"Kids need to understand that a rupture in a relationship does not mean the end of the relationship," says Julie Foster, LISW-S, RN, and an outpatient therapist for adolescents. "There are some very good outcomes to having an argument in front of your kids… Kids need to understand that people often disagree on things and can still be in a healthy and happy relationship. Kids also need to learn that just because someone is mad at them, it doesn't mean the relationship is over. Or that the other person will stop loving them."[4]

And continuing with the theme of transparency, never disregard the importance of making up in front of your child (even babies). When parents have calm disagreements and resolve any conflict in front of their children, it can help those kids develop better social skills, increased self-esteem, and greater respect for other perspectives.[5]

Ultimately, you're teaching them that finding your way through a conflict is sometimes more important than the conflict itself. Of course, depending upon the extent of how you make up, some things are better left private… but you get the point.

TRUST

All that being said, if you want a home where everyone is comfortable making mistakes, you must create an environment where everyone feels safe enough to let down their guard. But that requires trust. It's almost impossible to be fully accountable and transparent without it, which often funnels down from the top. Within a home, that means that it's up to you and your co-parent to create that safe space by modeling an environment of mutual trust — which is often easier said than done.

I once had a dad confess that he was struggling after his co-parent agreed to be in charge of ensuring there's always a surplus of diapers when needed. She did a great job at first (reordering when supply got low), but then simply got consumed with other things and dropped the ball.

Her lack of consistency not only hurt the trust built between them, but it also put her reliability into question. After the first time, he said it was no big deal, but a week later when his baby had a blowout and there were no diapers available, that was no longer the case.

From that point on, he began double-checking everything his co-parent was responsible for — which is never a good look for anyone involved. Luckily, after acknowledging her mistake and vowing to be more consistent, things soon went back to normal, though it did take a beat to rebuild that trust.

Consistency is crucial to building trust. A lack of consistency creates double the work and leaves everyone feeling frustrated. If you want to build a home where everyone has the freedom to chart their own path, you must begin with mutual trust. And to accomplish that goal:

Your word must be mighty!

Now, if you feel you and your co-parent already trust one another implicitly — great! However, for many parents (whether new to the game or not), building a strong foundation of mutual trust is one of the most difficult elements of parenting. And life with a newborn can slowly challenge that trust on a regular basis.

Hopefully, the guidance provided in this book will go a long way in helping you on your journey, but we are all human and therefore often come with baggage that pre-dates the arrival of our child. Just because two people were able to make a baby together (and may feel a strong connection to one another) does not guarantee they will completely trust one another with the well-being of a fragile newborn.

Gatekeeping

The time has come to introduce a common term in the parenting world that has created complications in innumerable homes throughout the years: Maternal Gatekeeping. The concept was popularized by a 1999 study from Sarah Allen and Alan Hawkins of Brigham Young University.[6] In essence, this is when one parent attempts to appoint themselves ruler within the home, and works to control every aspect of household responsibilities, including interactions with their child. This mentality is often then cemented by a co-parent (stereotypically a dad in previous generations) repeating tropes like: "Ask my wife, she's the boss," or "I don't know, ask your mom."

However, don't be fooled. Although maternal gatekeeping is more commonly associated with moms, it is entirely possible for a parent of any gender to take on these dangerous habits. It's typically whoever holds the more dominant role within the home. In our house, I was unfortunately that parent, which is why we will simply refer to it as gatekeeping* from here on out.

As the self-proclaimed gatekeeper, I quickly learned that the more control I asserted, the less confident my co-parent felt… and the less help I received.

In full transparency, the story I told at the beginning of this chapter about a parent who was so terrified of making a mistake that they were almost completely paralyzed on the parenting front — well, that was my co-parent. And I accept a good amount of the fault. In short, my actions were only hurting the both of us.

But let's back up a bit.

Gatekeeping often occurs when one parent feels unsupported in the home, while also lacking trust in the abilities of their co-parent (or in some cases, anyone else's abilities with regards to their family). Gatekeeping can also occur when one parent is working a paid job with responsibilities that fall outside the home, while their co-parent is working as a stay-at-home caregiver, and often feels isolated and powerless in the outside world. Therefore, the co-parent who feels powerless might assert their authority within the home (i.e. gatekeeping) in an attempt to justify their value to the world — declaring the home as *their* sole domain with statements like: "You're doing it wrong," or "It'll just be easier if I do it myself."

Unfortunately, that gatekeeper can then often find themselves feeling overburdened by the responsibilities they laid upon their own shoulders, while simultaneously resenting their co-parent's lack of involvement — even though they may have unknowingly been a huge barrier to that involvement.

MYTH #6 – THERE'S NO ROOM FOR MISTAKES AS A PARENT

If any of this sounds familiar to you, please know that you are in very good company. I have never led a dads group where the topic of gatekeeping did not come up in some form. It's quite a common issue between co-parents.

Research over the past two decades shows a direct correlation between how controlling gatekeepers are with regards to their partner's parenting, and how much parenting their partner is actually willing to take on.[7] The more gatekeeping from one parent, the less parental involvement from the other (which, as previously mentioned, is exactly what happened in our home).

The ideal way to combat this is to nip it in the bud before it ever becomes a problem in your home. By creating a united front from the moment you learn you're going to be parents, you can work to communicate and share responsibilities from the get-go.

"Whenever there is a problem, whether the water heater is broken or the house isn't clean, remember that it's not you versus your significant other versus the problem," says Shannon Carpenter, author of *The Ultimate Stay-at-Home Dad*. "It's you AND your spouse versus the problem. Whatever that happens to be."[8]

Now, for those that find themselves co-parenting with someone showing gatekeeper tendencies, you might first try vocalizing to your co-parent how it makes you feel when they gatekeep — as opposed to the more common response, which is to push down those feelings until you eventually blow up at them (which again, rarely solves anything).

I was truly oblivious about how my behavior was undermining my co-parent until she finally expressed her concerns. And truth be told, it didn't fix the issue overnight. But it did open the lines of communication in a way that allows her to speak up if my actions are ever making her feel obsolete.

And if you find that you are the one doing the gatekeeping (and kudos to you just for acknowledging it!), I highly recommend allowing yourself some extended time outside of the home with no responsibilities. I had actually been putting off a trip with some high school friends for quite some time. So I wrangled the group together and planned a long weekend away. And it was just what the doctor ordered. Although it was admittedly difficult to walk out the door, it forced me to relinquish control, which ultimately benefited everyone involved. It reminded me that I am a human who deserves a break from time-to-time. It also empowered my co-parent to take the reins, proving that she could, in fact, handle whatever got thrown her way (even if it wasn't always exactly how I would have handled it — we'll delve more into this in Myth #8).

MYTH #6 – THERE'S NO ROOM FOR MISTAKES AS A PARENT

But to successfully implement any of these strategies, you and your co-parent will need one crucial thing: TRUST (which brings us back full circle to the topic at hand).

The sooner you can build a strong foundation of mutual trust, the sooner you can combat any signs of gatekeeping within your home. Trust leads to an open environment to let down your walls. The freedom to be vulnerable and transparent. To express any needs or fears. And admit to any mistakes made while taking full accountability.

IN CLOSING

The secret no one will tell you is that much of life as a parent centers around trial and error. If you want to find a solution to any issue that may arise, you must be willing to fall on your face — in reality, it will happen whether you want it to or not. That's all part of the game of parenting, and mistakes are a big part of that process.

So, rather than attempting to avoid conflict with your co-parent (which will eventually erupt in some other fashion), why not try a more transparent approach by communicating your feelings while keeping your cool. At a minimum, it will create a less confusing environment for your little one, who will often sense any tension present — leaving them more room to enjoy their childhood, rather than navigate the ups and downs of your relationship.

The key is creating an environment with full accountability, transparency, and trust in order to ensure that mistakes are seen as no big thang. The real focus should be taking the time to learn from each and every one of them. We are *all* winging it when we first start out — that's where the adventure begins!

And like everything in life: *Practice Makes Progress.*

I think there's no better way to end this chapter than with my favorite quote by Samuel Beckett,[9] one that has gotten me through countless face plants — reminding me to simply dust myself off and jump back in the game:

"Ever tried? Ever failed?

No Matter. Fail again.

Fail better."

MYTH #7

YOU WILL NEVER HAVE SEX AGAIN

This myth will primarily apply to those with a romantic connection to their co-parent, but fear that connection has been lost as of late. It goes hand-in-hand with a number of other statements that people sometimes (obnoxiously) tell new parents — for example:

 Get ready for your life to be over.

OR

 Get ready for your partner to hate you.

Both of which honestly say more about *their* mental state than an actual foretelling of *your* future. The fact is that there will be an inevitable change in your relationship dynamic once a baby enters the scene, but that does not have to be a bad thing.

This chapter is where much of what we have discussed comes full circle. The most important thing to note is that once you become co-parents, your relationship will be heavily impacted by the choices you each make as individuals. In other words, your actions will have a huge influence on whether or not you find your groove again.

Let me clarify: once you have a kid together, you become forever bonded as business partners with a hyperfocus on your first, newly released co-venture. This added load of responsibility leaves co-parents with two options:

> *Option 1:* You can allow this new stress and weight of responsibility to drive a wedge between you and your partner.

OR

> *Option 2:* You can make the choice to be a team, where you each support one another as a united front — creating an even stronger bond than you had previously.

I'm not saying that Option 2 will be easy or won't come without its own stressors, but it's clearly the better option, no?!

MYTH #7 – YOU WILL NEVER HAVE SEX AGAIN

In full transparency, my partner and I (and countless other parents) unfortunately fell into Option 1, and it was not a fun road to go down. On the bright side, the path we took on our way to Option 2 is what inspired much of this chapter. The point is to say that we're all human, and co-parenting is tough.

So, how does this relate to sex?

Well, if the answer isn't already obvious, the odds of any intimacy are highly unlikely with a wedge of irritation and resentment between you (i.e., Option 1). And by intimacy, I don't just mean sex. I mean any sense of connection as two adults — which is where we'll be focusing our attention.

Once a baby enters the picture, you may find yourself in the same predicament as many new dads, which can often extend far beyond the fourth trimester: *Your co-parent is just not that into you.*

Perhaps it just feels that way. Or it might be true. But, do not believe for one moment that this has to be your new normal.

It takes work to rebuild that connection once a baby arrives. Your co-parent might need some space. Hell, you both might. That's one of the benefits of Freedom Shifts! Becoming a parent requires a major adjustment period for all parties involved. However, if you take the steps necessary to actively pursue Option 2 and work as a united front, the tide will very likely shift to your desired endgame (which is what this chapter is all about).

A Quick Heads-Up

Before we dive into those steps, it's important to note that your journey to maintaining a strong connection with your co-parent truly begins from the moment you become parents. With so much of your attention focused on your little one, it's possible the last thing on your mind is taking the time to think of things from your co-parent's perspective.

Assuming you are both new parents, the truth is that you might share many of the same unspoken anxieties and frustrations. However, if your co-parent gave birth, there's one major difference between the two of you — your physical body was never involved in the equation (aside from the initial act that launched this whole adventure in the first place).

Not only did they carry the baby for almost a year of their life, but they also had to then extract the baby from their body — by any means necessary. While labor can last anywhere from a matter of hours to days, recovery from the trauma that is childbirth can take much longer. The

MYTH #7 – YOU WILL NEVER HAVE SEX AGAIN

American Academy of Family Physicians (AAFP) points out that regardless of whether your co-parent had an easy or complicated delivery, whether they had a cesarean birth (C-section) or vaginal delivery, their body still went through a trauma and will need time to recover. In fact, a full recovery could take months. According to the AAFP, while a majority of birthing moms feel somewhat physically recovered by 6-8 weeks, it could take *much* longer to feel like themselves again.[1]

Moreover, although sex with your partner might be the last thing on either of your minds when you first become parents, her reasons likely extend far beyond feeling exhausted or overwhelmed. For many birthing moms, the physical transformation of the body that occurs post-birth can create a number of additional emotional obstacles to intimacy.

According to the Mayo Clinic (and many of the birthing parents I've interviewed through the years), there can be fear that the sex will hurt[2] — it's not like her body just got a small paper cut. Even more so, as if the strain of carrying a baby and giving birth are not enough, there's often the exhausting task of breastfeeding or pumping, which could leave your co-parent feeling more like a factory than a human being. My wife hated if I got anywhere near her breasts during the first few months of our child's life, as she had a difficult time not associating them with feeding our baby.

All of this confusion can understandably leave your co-parent feeling like their body is no longer their own. Therefore, it's not surprising that some might feel a need for physical space when the baby is sleeping (and a potential window for intimacy opens up), but that will not necessarily last forever *if* the appropriate steps are taken.

So, without further ado…

FORMULA FOR RE-CONNECTION

No matter the specifics of your situation — whether your partner gave birth, you're in a same-sex couple, or you became parents through surrogacy or adoption — becoming a parent will bring about a laundry list of changes to your lives. Aside from building a strong foundation of mutual trust (as discussed in Myth #6), the following are three additional suggestions to better support and understand one another — building an even stronger connection with your co-parent than you ever felt before.

Step 1:
Make Time to Clear the Air

When was the last time you asked how your co-parent was feeling... and then took the time to listen to their response? I mean truly listen, allowing them the space to vocalize any pent-up feelings or concerns — no matter how uncomfortable it may make you feel.

Moreover, when was the last time *you* were asked?!

Or the last time you asked yourself?

> *"Two monologues do not make a dialogue"*
> – Jeff Daley[3]

If you can't recall the answer, you're in pretty good company. You'd be shocked how few co-parents (and couples in general) take the time to ask one another, or even themselves, the simple question: "How are you feeling?"

If those kinds of conversations are rare in your home, it's time to ask yourself, *Why?* Maybe the thought to ask never crossed either of your minds. Maybe you each just assumed everything was fine (but you know what they say about assumptions). Or maybe you were each simply scared of the answer you might receive.

Regardless of the reason, the longer the question is avoided, the more potential damage the answer can cause to your connection with your co-parent and your home in general.

I understand that life with a newborn can be overwhelming and exhausting, and the last thing on your mind is asking one another about your feelings. But that simple question is one of the most important pieces to rebuilding a connection with one another.

Unfortunately, for many new parents, your co-parent can easily become the scapegoat for any and all frustrations.

The best thing you can do for your relationship is build a safe space to speak freely regarding any feelings you may be experiencing (whether positive or negative)... without judgment.

However, please know that the conversation must go both ways. As previously mentioned, I'm not a big fan of the extremely dated mentality of "happy wife, happy life," which implies that a man's feelings don't matter as long as his partner is happy. Disregarded feelings will only amount to much bigger problems down the line that often manifest in a way that is not healthy for anyone.[4]

From the multitude of co-parents I've spoken with through the years, I've found that the best way to check-in with one another is by implementing a *Weekly Business Meeting** *(WBM)*.

I know that may sound a bit formal or even intimidating to some. But rather than making every night about the business of parenting (filled with reminders and to-dos), the concept is to set aside some weekly one-on-one time to tackle all the business you can, including an emotional check-in.

The result? Six remaining days of the week with more opportunities for bonding — both with your baby and one another. It also opens the door for more Freedom Shifts, which benefits everyone.

WBMs are a time to reassess any previously agreed-upon Scope of Work and divide up any new tasks for the upcoming week. A time to review your calendar, do some meal planning, discuss your shopping list, or whatever other family business is monopolizing your minds. It's also a time to confess any responsibilities that might be tipping either of you over the edge. A time to reassess the best path forward to divide and conquer, so no one is left asking: "Is there anything I can do to help?"

Additionally, WBMs are a great opportunity to lay out any personal or professional goals for the week ahead. You can also share any personal wins either of you may have experienced that week. In fact, research shows that discussing positive experiences can lead to "increased overall life satisfaction, and even more energy."[5] And who doesn't want that?!

I know this might sound like a lot of work to some. The truth is that maintaining a connection with your co-parent will take work and may add more to your plate. But anything of value takes work!

Most importantly, think of this as a chance to sit down with your co-parent and discuss whatever it is that either of you feels the need to share — even if that's frustration with one another. Oftentimes, the best way to move forward is to simply release any past issues that might be holding us back. It's highly unlikely that you'll be able to act as a united front if there's loads of tension between you. And the best way to alleviate any tension is allowing the space for you each to feel heard — especially if you find yourself in what feels like a vicious cycle.

Early on after launching my podcast, I invited my wife to hop on the mic to discuss an argument we were having — mid fight.[6] It was a bold move, but It led to an extremely vulnerable (and cathartic) conversation which launched *DILF*'s popular "Co-Parenting Series[#]." By the end of the episode, we quickly realized that what we were arguing about had nothing to do with the situation before us. It wasn't about a lack of love. It was remnants from past feelings that had yet to be resolved and simply lingered silently, growing momentum in a way that could slowly poison any relationship — but especially dangerous for the often strained relationship between co-parents.

In short, we were each simply angry about other unresolved issues and using random arguments to vent frustrations without actually addressing the true issue at hand. But it was beginning to impact the environment in which we raised our son, and we needed to do something about it — which is how the concept of a weekly check-in (i.e. WBM) was born.

 #Use the QR code here to check out DILF's Co-Parenting Series

It took some time to perfect the formula but we found that beginning each WBM with some mutual compliments regarding the previous week helped to bring down our walls and set the stage for a more vulnerable and productive meeting. We also found that when it came time for the "emotional check-in" portion of our WBM, there's a big difference between a bitchfest and expressing one's feelings. And the major difference is how vulnerable you're willing to get with your feelings — the more "I" statements the better (e.g., "I feel very alone" or "I miss you"). In short, vulnerability begets vulnerability. Calm begets calm. When you show your co-parent respect, they will often return the favor.

But again, the most crucial piece to any successful WBM is that you are each given the space to express whatever it is you are feeling, while taking the time to *listen* to one another. In truth, this is one of the most crucial aspects for any healthy co-parenting relationship — but especially a romantic one.

Weekly Business Meeting – The Breakdown

If you want to try implementing a WBM — especially if it feels like a lot of irritations or frustrations have built up — it might benefit each of you to do a personal check-in prior to meeting. You can try journaling or talking to an impartial friend (or even a therapist). This will give you the chance to get all the "crap" out before you unload it onto one another, as well as gain some perspective from another person who might have dealt with something similar.

A personal check-in also allows the chance to *choose your battles** — more on this in the next chapter, but in essence, lay out all the things that are bothering you before you speak with your co-parent. You can then select the most pressing issue to discuss in your WBM. Bringing too many issues to the table in one meeting will likely overwhelm, and will rarely offer any meaningful resolution.

Suggested Agenda for each WBM

1) *Self-Acknowledged Wins:*

   Share any personal or parenting wins for the week.

2) *Three Compliments:*

   Take turns sharing three compliments for each other from the past week. This will help you to lower defenses, while reminding each of you all the wonderful things you appreciate about one another.

3) *Emotional Check-In:*

Each of you should be given the time to speak about whatever you are feeling without interruptions. (My wife and I even go so far as to cover our mouths to avoid spitting out defensive reactions.) Being given the space to fully vent whatever you might be feeling, with no one interrupting, often allows one to organically calm themselves.

REMEMBER, good behavior begets good behavior — so, lead by example: Be the DILF you want to see in the world!

4) *Review Responsibilities:*

Discuss the practical business of the upcoming week. Reassess the balance of household and parenting responsibilities and determine if any changes are needed.

5) *Goal Setting + Freedom Shift Planning:*

Take a moment of silence to each jot down any goals for the upcoming week, whether personal or professional. Then, assign one night in the upcoming week for each of you to take a Freedom

Shift. Ideally with one additional night for a Joint Freedom Shift (i.e., a date night — even if it's just some quality time after your baby falls asleep).

Homework

Prepare for your next WBM the same way you did your first — especially if there are any issues that are still lingering. Tackle whatever tasks you agreed to take on, and try your darndest to keep to the goals you set for the week. And if it's hard for you to find the time to work through any remaining feelings or frustrations, then allow an hour prior to your next WBM for journaling. This will help you to clear your head and come in fresh.

Sometimes, the most productive WBMs are the ones where co-parents simply take the time to acknowledge each other's feelings. Feeling heard is the first step to healing any past emotional wounds, and a major step on the voyage to (re)building a strong connection.

The simple act of hearing another person out — without reacting — can do wonders in clearing the air. You might also find that the feelings expressed are more common than you realize, and the mere act of speaking them aloud makes you each feel refreshed.

After all, communication is one of the key components to building an organic connection, which is paramount if you have any intention of getting back to a place of intimacy.

Step 2:
Sharing the Load

We've touched on this previously, but if you are craving more intimacy with your co-parent, another crucial step is attempting to put yourselves in their shoes. There's no need to wait for your WBM to jump in and handle a task that needs doing — especially if you notice your co-parent is feeling overburdened. Again, carrying your share of the mental load is thinking ahead about things that need to get tackled and doing them *before* they pile up or cause an issue.

A 2008 survey of over 50k married couples found that "most of the couples (81%) where both spouses perceived the relationship as equalitarian were happily married, while most of the couples (82%) where both spouses perceived their relationship as traditional [i.e., an unequal balance of responsibilities] were mainly unhappy."[7]

Obviously, it's up to each individual couple to decide what they perceive as an equitable partnership, but in the end, it mostly comes down to taking the time and effort needed to share the weight of responsibility so neither co-parent feels regularly overburdened.

If you're looking to plant the seeds of a healthy partnership (especially during the fourth trimester), there is no better way than providing as much support as you are able to give. If either of you isn't feeling supported, then any healthy opportunities for connection often go right in the trash with the dirty diapers.

The more you have one another's back, the less over-burdened you will each feel. And that means more room available for connection — which can lead to more intimacy.

Step 3:
Quality Time

One of the biggest complaints amongst new parents is that they often feel more like business partners than lovers, or worse, two ships passing in the night. One of the best decisions you can make as a new parent is to carve out some quality time with your co-parent (separate from your WBM) — a time to reconnect and have some carefree fun.

If a trusted friend or family member is willing to watch the baby for an hour, go for a walk together. If someone you trust can watch the baby a bit longer, go grab a bite to eat outside of the house and make it a date night! If you can't find someone, try grabbing a deck of cards and playing a few rounds of whatever game suits your fancy. Anything you can do together that takes your minds off the business of parenting counts.

I cannot stress enough how important it is to make your relationship with your co-parent a priority. I know time can be limited, but this is more about quality over quantity. A little quality time is better than none at all. And to ensure that time is utilized to its fullest potential, you might even try eliminating your devices from the equation. I would even go so far as to recommend you keep your phone out of your bedroom at night to create a more relaxed environment, as well as increasing any opportunities for organic connection.

It's worked wonders in our home, but it admittedly took a beat to iron out logistics. If you use baby-related apps (such as a digital monitor or tracking apps), you could try keeping a separate device like an old iPhone in the bedroom. Then, load it with only essential tools — from an alarm and music to any crucial apps relating to your little one. In other words: no email, messaging apps, or social media. I know this may feel like a harsh truth for some, but unless you're a doctor on call, if your co-parent and baby are within earshot, is your phone really that much of a necessity?!

After introducing this concept on the podcast, many couples reached out to express how much this simple change not only helped them to sleep more soundly, but also allowed more space for intimate conversations with their co-parent and opportunities for connection.

The choice is yours, but if you choose to give it a try, it may also be a way to set some solid boundaries with work. Studies show that excessive smartphone usage can make you more irritable and less available to the needs of your family, not to mention its impact on your personal mental well-being.[8]

Again, I'm not suggesting you throw your device out the window, I'm simply saying that the act of placing it outside your bedroom at night just might help to create a more sacred and calming space for your mind, your body, and your relationship with your co-parent. You can always doomscroll in the morning.

CO-SLEEPING

Now, on to one last controversial topic that could affect quality time with your co-parent: co-sleeping*. There are strong arguments on each side as to the benefits and disadvantages of sharing a room or bed with your child beyond the first few months. As with everything in parenting, much of this will come down to personal preference — I'm not here to judge your decisions.

On one hand, there's a reason the practice has been around for centuries; on the other hand, it could come at a price.[9] Since this book focuses on the mental health of parents, I will say that if co-sleeping means that you aren't getting any rest, or your relationship with your co-parent is suffering due to a lack of alone time — that's not good for anyone.

If you have the energy, that limited window after your little one goes down for the night (or as much of the night as the sleep g-ds will allow) is one of the best opportunities to share some "adult" time with your co-parent. It's a time to remind you that you are *more* than simply co-parents. It's a chance to reconnect, to laugh, or even just offer a no-strings attached massage — any opportunity for organic connection with no expectation or pressure for anything more.

At the very least, studies show that a minimum of a 10-second hug can release oxytocin[10] (aka the "love" hormone), which can do wonders in knocking down walls and rebuilding connections.

In summary, committing to some quality adult time will not only allow you each to feel more like a human, it might just help you rediscover that pre-baby magic.

IN CLOSING

Again, the reality of this myth will depend heavily on the choices you each make as co-parents. But know that the degree to which you and your partner support one another when you first become new parents will have a large impact on your future relationship dynamics.

Therefore, if you want any chance of strengthening your connection on the road back to intimacy, remember the formula:

1. Build a strong foundation of mutual trust
2. Allow opportunities for open communication
3. Do your part to share the load (both mental and physical)
4. Commit to some quality one-on-one time

I'd also recommend you consider re-reading this chapter *with* your co-parent. It might be extremely beneficial in validating whatever you each may be feeling, while bringing you together as you plan your next steps on the road to re-connection.

Of course, even if you work to follow all of the steps detailed above, there are no guarantees. Each relationship comes with its own unique set of circumstances. That said, it will stack the odds in your favor, and it is likely your best chance at reigniting any passion potentially missing from your relationship.

At a minimum, following these steps will pave the way for a stronger partnership. And as referenced in Myth #4, in the nearly 80-year Harvard Study of Adult Development, close relationships are the number one factor for men living healthier and more fulfilling lives.[11] If that's not enough, a stronger connection with your co-parent will also lay the foundation for a happier home, offering a safer environment for your child's growing mind and emotional well-being.[12]

MYTH #8

THERE IS ONLY ONE CORRECT WAY TO DO THINGS

Logic tells us that this myth is clearly nonsense, as it is not the case with regards to anything in life (parenting or otherwise). Although, as a new parent, it can feel very true, as if one wrong move will screw up your child for life. If you've ever felt this way, you are far from alone. That feeling usually comes from not yet having found any other way to achieve your goal… yet.

The reality is that you don't have to do things the way your parents did, or the way your friends do, or even the way your co-parent does. In fact, attempting different approaches — and successfully implementing one — not only builds your confidence in your skills as a parent, but also helps to establish your independence from your co-parent. And that independence is crucial in your path to truly sharing responsibilities on the home front. Moreover, it can open the door to the discovery of techniques better customized for your unique family.

However, in order to build a home where this mentality is not only followed but celebrated, here are a few things to keep in mind:

RECOMMENDATION 1: LEARN YOUR KID

Back in the beginning of our pregnancy, I was hanging out with a friend when I heard his baby screaming from the other room. I was quite alarmed, but he was completely calm. When I asked if the baby was alright, he replied that the cry simply meant the baby was up from her nap.

"How do you know that?" I asked.

"Because of the cry," he replied.

I soon learned of the common belief that children (of all ages) have different cries for different situations, ranging from simply wanting some attention to a potentially serious injury.

The obvious next question was how the heck would I be able to differentiate? I immediately went to YouTube to search and try to memorize different baby cries. Luckily, the answer became quite clear once my baby was born:

Every child is different

Now, I can't say if this "cry theory" is universally true, because again, every baby is different. I found it to be true with my child (as did everyone I've ever interviewed), but the specifics of what each cry means will be specific to each child... and then translated by those who know them best. You may not get it right every time, but like everything in parenting, there is no better teacher than hands-on experience.

One of the most important jobs we all have as parents is learning your babies' cries, likes & dislikes, and personal preferences. Building upon the concept of dedicated focus from Myth #3, you have to allow the time and space to get to know *your* baby — in other words: *Learn Your Kid**.

Newborns are extremely adaptable, but they also can have innate preferences — especially when it comes to feeding, burping or calming techniques (the primary skills needed for new parents). I am not saying that *any* child is set in their ways from day one, nor that any initial preferences will remain the same forever. But attempting to force them to do something they are not open to doing (like with any individual on the planet) will rarely end well.

Even in those early weeks when they hardly *feel* like humans, babies still have minds of their own. They may not be able to use words, but I assure you that when they do not like something, they will make it abundantly clear.

MYTH #8 — THERE IS ONLY ONE CORRECT WAY TO DO THINGS

"Remember that the brain is a survival organ. It needs consistent feeding, consistent interaction, lots of looking and cues. You should understand the emotional landscape and repertoire of your baby better than you understand your own stock portfolio."[1]

— Dr. John Medina, a developmental molecular biologist & author of *Brain Rules for Baby: How to Raise a Smart and Happy Child from Zero to Five.*

So, what's the best way to Learn Your Kid?

I recommend an approach called dedicated observation* — based on a technique Montessori teachers use.[2] In essence, regularly allow yourself to be fully present with your child while attempting to follow three simple rules:

- Eliminate all distractions (including any mobile devices) for at least 25 minutes
- Sit with your baby with no other agenda than watching them interact with the world
- Be available, be patient, and stay the course!

Some of my favorite memories during the first year of my child's life are just lying on the floor in the nursery with some calming music while quietly getting to know him — taking note of how he responded to various toys, music and people. Sometimes my in-laws would even FaceTime us and tune in like it was an episode of *The Truman Show*.

Becoming a dedicated observer is not only beneficial in learning more about your child, but also for your own mental well-being as a new parent. It can be quite a calming experience to eliminate all distractions and allow the space to simply be available to your little one. "Parents are a child's best toy, " attests Gladys Atawo, manager of child health and development at Toronto Public Health.[3]

Dedicated observation can eventually make you an expert translator with regards to your child's preferences and needs, while simultaneously helping to secure your bond as a stable constant in their world.

RECOMMENDATION 2: REMAIN OPEN

To be clear, believing that there is more than one way to do something does not mean you should ignore every successful technique used by others. The key is remaining available to other options, while reserving judgment — admittedly, no easy task.

I am, of course, not saying that you must use every piece of advice offered, but that doesn't mean that you shouldn't be open-minded enough to hear (at least some of) it.

People have been parenting (and surviving) since the beginning of time. And although circumstances may vary, it's quite likely that no matter what situation you are dealing with, someone has already gone through something quite similar and found a way through it to a successful outcome.

I think most would agree that one of the best ways to achieve any goal is to do your research, which involves keeping your eyes and ears open to what has worked for others in similar situations. Then, simply drop the things that don't apply to you or your family, and retain the advice that does.

The one thing that can often get in the way of even the best advice is the tone with which it is presented. Sometimes advice is offered in a tone that is simply too condescending to handle. Sometimes, you just dislike the person giving the advice and your pride won't allow you to hear it.

The best thing you can do is think of every piece of advice offered as another option in your parenting toolkit. And in truth, simply listening exerts a lot less energy than fighting back in irritation.

One example that comes to mind was when our baby was one month old. My wife and I each admitted that we were feeling a bit trapped in our home. In response, an old friend (with older kids) randomly mentioned that the newborn stage was a great time to do some light traveling. At first, we dismissed this as a crazy concept. But after letting it settle in, we decided that some easy travel might be a good option — it was at least worth a try! After all, there was a good chance our baby would sleep through a short car ride. And what did it matter where we were, as long as we had everything we needed to feed, change, and put our baby to sleep. Yes, the logistics (and the packing) could get a bit tricky, but it seemed to us that the benefits outweighed the hassle.

So, we tried it, and headed from Los Angeles to San Diego for the weekend — and it was wonderful. It wasn't perfect, but it rejuvenated us in a way that we each desperately needed. It also built our confidence, learning that we didn't need everything to be perfect in order to survive and even thrive as parents.

Of course, a suggestion like this always comes down to personal preference, as well as your specific family dynamics and kid. However, knowing that there are options other than locking yourself in your home for months with a newborn can be nice to hear, *if* you're open to hearing it.

In the end, whether you take anyone's advice is entirely up to you and your co-parent. I believe the best approach is to view every piece of advice as pure research. You don't have to agree or be offended by it — they're just options. And allowing yourself to take it all in does not equate to you agreeing to anything. Trust your instincts. It's up to you to gauge what advice is worth utilizing, but never underestimate the benefits of remaining open-minded to the wisdom of those who came before you.

RECOMMENDATION 3:
STAY IN SYNC WITH YOUR CO-PARENT

I once had a parent tell me that when they're not on the same page with their co-parent, they simply agree to their co-parent's methods — in essence, giving their word that they will follow the same path — but then do things their own way when their co-parent isn't looking.

Although not that uncommon, this is a dangerous mentality that will immediately poison any trust that's been built between co-parents (or partners in any given situation). You don't need to do things the exact same way your co-parent does, but you should both agree on the desire to try different approaches. It might take some cojones to speak up and voice an alternate perspective, but it's better than what will happen when that parent inevitably gets "caught" going against their word.

Every time trust is broken, those walls that prevent us from being vulnerable (and open to hearing another's perspective) only get stronger and harder to knock down. And where does that leave two co-parents working to build a united front?

This mentality might also bite you each in the tush as your

MYTH #8 — THERE IS ONLY ONE CORRECT WAY TO DO THINGS

child gets older. Kids can always smell when parents aren't on the same page. And that lack of unity is the recipe for a child who pins parents against one another, refusing to listen to any boundaries set by either of you.

While we've already established that it's okay to do things differently, you should agree upon some basic parameters that you both vow to follow when it comes to your child.

But in order to achieve this, you may need to rely heavily upon a principle we mentioned briefly in the last chapter: choose your battles. It's a way to rethink disagreements before they rev up. Just pause and ask yourself if this is really a road you want to go down.

The truth is that your time is often quite limited as a parent, so you need to be careful about where you exert your energy. When you have a difference of opinion, it doesn't mean you are not correct, but it also doesn't mean your co-parent's point has no validity. The most important thing is to find some common ground and move forward together.

If you battle over every issue that comes up, you will never have any peace — nor will your baby. Therefore, it's important for you and your co-parent to target the issues that cause the most strife in your relationship, as well as any issues that jump out as extremely important to either of you. Then, settle upon a short list of unbreakable rules that you both agree to follow. Ideally, these center around the safety of your child, but often extend to situations that make either of you truly uncomfortable.

Once you settle upon that short list of mutually agreed-upon, steadfast rules — I like to call them your *Agreed-Upon Parameters** — you should then allow one another the freedom to find your own way within them.

For example, I recently spoke to co-parents who were arguing over the best way to burp their baby. They each preferred very different techniques and insisted that their way was best. I suggested that maybe they were missing the point. If both techniques worked (which they did), then maybe the specific technique used was not as important as the common goal: the Agreed-Upon Parameter that the baby must be burped after every feeding.

Some even believe that utilizing different techniques helps your child to become more adaptable. And allowing the space for you each to discover your own techniques will only create more options. You truly never know what methods will work until you try — again, much of parenting really comes down to trial and error. But one thing's for sure — the more effort you make to remain on the same page with your co-parent regarding your Agreed-Upon Parameters, the more freedom you should each feel to find your sea legs and successfully explore your own way of doing things.

MYTH#8 — THERE IS ONLY ONE CORRECT WAY TO DO THINGS

RECOMMENDATION 4: OWN YOUR PART

Once you Learn Your Kid, do your research, and agree upon the fundamentals — while allowing for flexibility within them — it's important that you fully own whatever tasks you agree to take on. This applies to anything that falls within your agreed-upon Scope of Work or during any time period when your co-parent is on a Freedom Shift.

In short, whoever is on duty needs to accept full responsibility for the task at hand. And remember that preparation is your friend on the road to success.

A dad in one of my new-dad groups once told me a story about an experience he had during a late-night feed. He had agreed to handle the night shift but then had a drink (or two) and passed out next to his sleeping co-parent once his baby went down. He had set an alarm to do a dream feed, but unfortunately slept through it. He was then awoken by his annoyed co-parent with a pillow to the face when the baby began screaming in the night. Obviously not the ideal way to wake up, but he had agreed to take on the night shift, and that involved anything the baby needed during that time, including any feedings.

He immediately ran to his crying baby and took her to the kitchen to prepare a bottle. The baby was not pleased. He went to the fridge to grab some breastmilk, but there was none in sight, so he grabbed a frozen bag to thaw while attempting to rock his baby. Once thawed, he poured the milk into a bottle, but it spilled everywhere. Since he and his co-parent had agreed to add some formula into the mix, he then took that route, but his baby was pretty pissed by this point and would not calm down to take the bottle once it was ready. In frustration, he then tried jamming the bottle into the baby's mouth, which (not shockingly) did not work. Finally, he gave up, woke his co-parent, and asked if she would breastfeed. In no time, she calmed the baby and fed her with ease.

The whole experience left him feeling like a failure. And it didn't help that his co-parent now seemed to no longer trust him with the night shift and insisted on handling it. Due to his work schedule, he had little time with his baby during the day, and now, without the night shift, he found himself with limited bonding time — which left him feeling distanced from both his co-parent and his baby. He was also now having trouble sleeping due to the whole situation, so neither he nor his co-parent were getting any solid rest.

After we spoke, he went to his co-parent, vulnerably

MYTH #8 – THERE IS ONLY ONE CORRECT WAY TO DO THINGS

acknowledged his mistakes, and asked if she would trust him with another chance at the night shift. She agreed. That night, after his co-parent went to bed, he was ready. No alcohol, no earplugs, no sleeping pills that could make him sleep so deeply that his co-parent would have to wake him when it was time to feed. He simply prepped a bottle so it was good to go for the dream feed. He then grabbed a book and waited patiently. When it came time for the feeding, he gently picked up his little one, calmly fed her the pre-prepped bottle, and then put her back down to bed seamlessly. When he got back into bed, his co-parent flipped over and snuggled him until they both fell back asleep.

This is all to say that truly owning whatever task you agree to take on requires patience and follow-through. And that includes any prep work you can do to set yourself up for success. The fact is that so much of life with a newborn (and parenting in general) is out of our control, so why not do whatever is within your power to sway the odds in your favor.

This will not only allow you the time (and brain space) to explore different tactics in the moment, but also show your co-parent that you can be trusted with any task that falls in your court. And vice versa.

IN CLOSING

One of the most unforgettable quotes I ever heard came from a *DILF* interview[4] I did with Abner Ramirez of the band, Johnnyswim (a personal favorite of mine). Inspired by the words of Dr. John Medina, Abner said,

> "The best thing you can do to maximize your children's ability to grow and learn ... is to go home and love your wife well. If your kids see that, that's the environment in which they will grow to their greatest capacity."

He then went on to share the associated philosophy he lives by with his children:

> "Regardless of what you see in this wild world — me and Mom are a unit ... even if we argue or disagree or see things differently. This ship has two captains, but we will steer in one direction ... and that is not up for debate."

The thing I love most about this sentiment is the acknowledgement that a true united front requires two individuals — each with differing opinions and perspectives — to come together and find a common ground. And to achieve this, co-parents will need to allow one another the

MYTH #8 – THERE IS ONLY ONE CORRECT WAY TO DO THINGS

freedom to find their own way while journeying towards the same destination.

Even after reading this chapter, you might still run into situations where it feels like there is only one way to accomplish any goal — likely because you haven't found another way that has worked. But when you encounter those situations, the most important thing you can do is trust yourself.

If you don't trust yourself, you won't have the confidence to hear the advice of others and choose the path that's best for your family. If you don't trust yourself, you won't be able to articulate your opinions or follow through with your word. And if you don't trust yourself, why would anyone else trust you, including your co-parent or your child?

> "We can't ask people to give to us something that we do not believe we're worthy of receiving."
> – Brene Brown[5]

Trusting yourself is the key to discovering your own path. It's the key to everything. Trusting yourself will give you the inner strength to take a deep breath when times get tough, and remember that there is always more than one way to achieve any goal.

MYTH #9

GOOD PARENTS *ALWAYS* PUT THEIR KID'S NEEDS FIRST

This is probably one of the most confusing myths of this book. And it makes sense. Ignoring the needs of our children feels selfish and wrong, but that's precisely what makes this myth so misunderstood. No one is implying that you should ignore the needs of your child. The issue is the concept of consistently putting the needs of your children *before* your own — as if doing so will earn you some kind of golden badge.

The best way to reframe this myth is to think about that classic rule stated before every flight you've ever taken:

"Please secure *your* oxygen mask first... before assisting others."

Why?

Because if the plane is going down and you run out of oxygen or pass out, you'll be no good to anyone — least of all your children. So, if your ultimate goal is helping them, doesn't it make sense that you should first look after your own well-being so that you actually have the capacity to accomplish your goal?

This may seem like an extreme example, but the principle still applies. If you are not taking care of yourself (both your physical and your emotional well-being), how helpful can you really be to your child, or anyone else for that matter? If you're exhausted, short-tempered, or even physically sick, can you honestly say you're capable of giving the support they need and deserve?

Of course, each and every child's needs are important (especially when that child is a helpless baby), but that doesn't eliminate the fact that every parent also deserves a break from time-to-time. In fact, it's crucial to the health of your baby. You need all your wits about you to act in the best interests of your child — that's another major motivation behind Freedom Shifts.

BALANCE

All that being said, like everything in life, there are always exceptions to the rule. If your child is sick or going through a difficult time, you'll likely need to prioritize their needs above all else. Sometimes your family needs you, and everything else has to wait. But other times you may have an emergency deadline and your income is on the line. When there are no other pressing issues on the home front, work may need to come first. Sometimes, you might find yourself feeling disconnected from your co-parent, and your relationship needs to come first. And sometimes, you may find yourself nearing a breaking point, and you must put *yourself* first. And there is nothing wrong with that. Simply having the capacity to acknowledge when you're nearing that point is one of the greatest examples you can provide for your child. Ideally, you can demonstrate the importance of taking time for yourself *prior* to hitting your breaking point.

When it comes down to it, parenting is all about ebbs and flows — it's about balancing your priorities. The concept of "all or nothing" is the true myth.

PERSONAL BOUNDARIES

Another crucial piece to combating this myth is the concept of *personal boundaries** — a line in the sand that you agree to never cross, while asking others (like your co-parent and loved ones) to do the same. These are similar to the theory of setting Agreed-Upon Parameters with your co-parent; however, personal boundaries take that concept one step further — they're rules you set for yourself to protect your physical, emotional, and mental well-being.

I briefly mentioned a great example of personal boundaries in Myth #5. During the first few months of my baby's life, I often found myself voluntarily sacrificing my Freedom Shift in order to "rescue" my co-parent when I heard her struggling in the morning with our little one. I thought I was being a hero — even though she never asked for the help. But I soon realized that rushing in to save the day was only hurting all of us. I was damaging her confidence in finding her own way, as well as hindering the connection she was working to build with our baby. And if that wasn't bad enough, I was giving up my Freedom Shift, so I wasn't getting the time needed to refill my cup and everyone was left feeling the yuck.

DILF Quick Hit

If you or your co-parent are struggling with how to avoid undermining your co-parent, you might consider checking out this popular *DILF Quick Hit* podcast episode.

Sacrificing a Freedom Shift to help your co-parent may not seem like a big deal at first, but patterns tend to solidify quickly during the early days of parenting. You may eventually feel the weight of your co-parent being constantly reliant on you to save the day — even if they truly aren't. Additionally, you may begin to resent them for it (even if they never explicitly asked for help). You may also become irritated when it's their Freedom Shift and they do not return the favor. By taking full advantage of your Freedom Shifts, you are actually helping set strong personal boundaries while doing both yourself and your co-parent a great service.

If the tables are turned and it's your co-parent coming to the rescue during their Freedom Shift, you could say something like, "I love you, but it's your turn to relax and take some much-deserved time for yourself. I got this." By expressing this aloud, you are not only allowing yourself the space to find your own way, but also setting a precedent for the importance of your co-parent's self-care (while setting the stage for you to do the same when it comes time for your Freedom Shift).

As your baby grows and life gets back to some form of new normal, personal boundaries will inevitably need to extend beyond the bubble of your homelife. One of the biggest areas in which I needed to set personal boundaries was with my phone. I know you may be thinking to yourself, *He's trying to take away my phone again?! Is this guy some kind of Luddite?* But hear me out: Have you ever found yourself reading an overwhelming email, and then avoid it by distracting yourself for the next twenty minutes in a mindless social media scroll? I know I have, and it never does much to help my anxiety, mood, or the issue at hand. In fact, I have found that consuming my thoughts with work to-do lists and the never-ending boomerang between emails, texts, social media and whatsapp can create a formula for disaster. A situation where I become so emotionally exhausted that I don't feel connected to anything — let alone my child. And what kind of role model can I be as a parent if I no longer recognize myself in the mirror?

Therefore, in our home, I have set a strict personal boundary when it comes to weekends. Unless there's a work emergency, I don't work on weekends. I work my tail off during the week, but then I'm off. And to ensure I follow through on my "work fast," I turn off my phone from Friday night to Sunday morning.

I disconnect in order to *reconnect* with my loved ones and myself.

This allows me the space to reset while stretching out my weekend (at least it feels that way). Most importantly, it ensures I have as much carefree family time as possible to recoup my energy and savor every precious moment the weekend has to offer.

I'm aware that this may feel too intimidating for some to tackle, and not possible for everyone. For instance, I would love if my co-parent also agreed to this personal boundary for herself, but turning off her phone all weekend is quite difficult for her. When she does, she always seems to feel lighter and more present, but our phones are an intense addiction. And as I can only control my own actions, I've made the decision to choose my battles on this one. It's not the hill I want to die on. I simply stick to *my* personal boundary — taking care of my own mental health — so I can be available for her if and when she needs me.

Boundary-Setting in Action

Another example that comes to mind regarding both balance and personal boundaries is a surprising story I heard during the second season of *DILF*. In the episode, I interviewed Dave Callaham, the co-writer behind Marvel's *Shang-Chi and the Legend of the Ten Rings*, as well as the Oscar-nominated *Spider-Man: Across The Spider-Verse*. This fellow dad and accomplished screenwriter discusses the personal boundary he set with executives from a high-profile movie studio when they scheduled a meeting that conflicted with his family's dinnertime ritual.[1]

In response, he told them he would need to be off the call by 5:30 p.m. as he cooks dinner every night and has his nightly bedtime ritual with his family. But when the time came, most of the executives were late to the call, which didn't actually start until around 5:20 p.m. So, he reminded them of the boundary he set, and when 5:30 arrived, he politely said goodbye.

"I just started to think: I don't want my daughter to remember any of this as, 'Dad wasn't around,' or 'Dad was too busy.' Anytime I can avoid that, I'm going to avoid that. And what I discovered was, you can avoid that a lot more than people seem to think you can," said Callaham.

The next day, one of his producers called and said, "You can't do that." But you know what ended up happening? Nothing. And from that moment on, the executives respected his time a lot more.

I know this approach may not work in every professional situation. It's up to each individual to decide how best to handle. But what I love about this example is the reminder that no matter who you are or what you do to make a living, balance is still crucial for every single individual on the planet.

Obviously, the concept of balance and personal boundaries will look different for each individual. For instance, Wharton organizational psychologist Adam Grant says:

> "The idea that work-life balance means 'I show up at 10 a.m. and I'm done by 3 p.m.' is ridiculous. The successful people I know don't tend to have very balanced days. They will have a whole day where all they do is work. But then the next day, all they do is spend time with their families."[2]

Sometimes the best solution is just remembering the principle of quality over quantity. There is nothing wrong with working your arse off during designated hours (and yes, these may vary at times), but then, outside of those hours, devote as much time as you can to yourself and your family — with no distractions. Even a single, uninterrupted hour can be more meaningful than three hours, half present, while constantly checking your phone or taking calls. Oftentimes, even just a short break can quickly put everything back into perspective, and ultimately introduce more joy into your daily life.

MIND-NUMBING VS. MIND-CALMING

There is one important caveat to clarify when it comes to prioritizing time for yourself. Be aware of the difference between mind-numbing* activities versus mind-calming* activities.

Mind-numbing activities might include binging junk food, doomscrolling, or excessive alcohol or substance abuse. These activities may pass the time as a way of avoiding whatever is causing you stress, but rarely do anything to ultimately relieve any of that stress.[3]

On the other hand, mind-calming activities tend to rejuvenate you, while giving you the space to address whatever it was that stressed you in the first place. My theory is that these activities — that ultimately better your life — usually involve some form of "connection."

To clarify, that connection could include a wide array of options:

- *Connection with yourself* (taking some dedicated me-time while on your Freedom Shift) — from some meditation to a quiet, relaxing bath or sauna.

- *Connection with your co-parent* — from a date night to dinner together after your baby goes to sleep.

- *Connection with your kid* — even while still on parenting duty, a nightly bedtime ritual and storytime can be an extremely calming and rejuvenating experience.
- *Connection with nature* — from a simple walk alone outside to some gardening.
- *Connection with your body* — from a solid workout to a stretch session.
- *Connection with an old friend* — grab a bite to eat with someone that makes you laugh, or kill two birds and go for a jog together.
- *Connection with your creative side* — from cooking something new to practicing a musical instrument. You can even grab a coloring book, which is scientifically proven to reduce activity in the amygdala, the part of the brain responsible for fight-or-flight stress response.[4]

As you can see, you have many options — in fact, why not take a moment to select one mind-calming activity to do right now. There's no better time to begin a new habit than the present!

IN CLOSING

As you may have gathered, one of the main themes of this book is that taking time for your own self-care is just as important as taking care of your little one. That said, I'd like to re-stress that taking care of your adult relationships is equally crucial. One of the biggest dangers I've noticed amongst new parents is consistently putting the needs of their child before the needs of their relationships with their friends and loved ones — especially their co-parent. If put on the back burner for too long, *any* relationship is bound to fall apart — as is any support system you may have already set in place.

As stated in the former U.S. Surgeon General's Advisory on the Mental Health & Well-Being of Parents, "Simply put, caregivers need care, too."[5]

As I mentioned in the introduction of this book, my decision to swallow my feelings and never focus any attention on my own needs was my downfall when I first became a parent. Again, there is nothing wrong with focusing a good amount of attention on your child — they need to know that they are loved and one of your top priorities. But we must also leave some room for ourselves, or we'll honestly be no good to anyone.

Modeling healthy behavior is how we teach our kids to develop and nurture their own happy and healthy relationships throughout their lives. In the end, neglecting ourselves or our relationships by putting the needs of our children above all else serves no one — least of all our children.

MYTH #10

YOU WILL LOVE *EVERY* MOMENT OF BEING A PARENT

When my kid was about nine months old, after pulling an all-nighter for work, I was awakened at 6 a.m. by him screaming from his crib. Normally this wouldn't have been the biggest issue because (as I've mentioned before) my co-parent usually handles mornings. However, on this particular day, my wife had an early meeting and was already out of the house, which meant I was on duty with less than two hours of sleep under my belt.

On top of that, my son was in a mood. Not only was this about an hour earlier than his usual wake-up time, but that morning he fully embodied the essence of "waking up on the wrong side of the bed." I tried to give him a bottle, but he rejected it. I tried to rock him back to the Point of Calm, but he squirmed out of my arms and defiantly laid himself on the floor. He then began peeking under the tiny crack of the closed bedroom door in what I can only assume was an attempt to find his mom through the small ray of light that shined through — as some form of relief from the "torture" of having to deal with me in the morning.

I get it, he was used to his mom in the morning, but I was too exhausted to deal with any of it. So I picked him up and walked him around the house to show him that no one else was home. It was either me or nada. Eventually, he accepted the bottle but did not want me involved. Instead, he insisted on holding it himself, and then dropped it — spilling milk everywhere. He then proceeded to fling his yogurt across the room. It was a complete disaster.

Once I finally got him dressed, with a crazy day of meetings ahead of me, we jumped in the car to head to daycare. And as we were driving, he started smiling at me in the mirror. He then began repeating the word, "Dada." And my heart just… melted. And once I dropped him off — after the shortest period of silent alone time — I missed him already.

And that, my friends, is parenthood.

The truth is, it's impossible to love every moment of *anything* in life. The brutal reality is that parenting is hard. At times, you may feel rejected, exhausted or even at your breaking point. But the one common denominator almost every parent will tell you (once you get past the BS) is that when it comes to parenting, the good — by far — outweighs any difficulties that arise throughout the journey.

So, when those tough times arise, just remember the famous adage: *This too shall pass.*

And to take that one step further, parenthood is certainly *not* the end of fun. I have had more fulfilling, spontaneous, unforgettable moments as a parent than I ever had before. It's just different.

There will, of course, be many other lessons that reveal themselves to you along the way, but think of this book as an ongoing mental health resource. A reminder of the importance of taking care of you. After all, if you are not taking care of yourself, it'll be hard to be available to the needs of your family. And it will make it especially difficult to enjoy the ride.

So, in an attempt to ensure your success, let's recap three of the most important areas to focus your attention:

1) TRUST IN YOURSELF

If something is off — or you're feeling isolated or lost — it's up to you to speak up. You must advocate for your own needs and the needs of your family. Always allow yourself the freedom to find your own path. Even if there were only one "right" way to do things as a parent (which is not the case), it takes time to discover what that best way is for *your* family.

Again, every child is unique, as is every family dynamic. So, avoid comparisons, and take the dedicated time to Learn Your Kid. And the best way to do that is to get involved as soon as possible in every way you can. Bonding comes from time put in. Be present. Make yourself available to interact and play, while eliminating distractions… and be patient. Becoming a dedicated observer will eventually make you an expert translator of your child's preferences, needs, and quirks. It will also secure your bond as a stable constant in their world, which is where the fun begins.

At the end of the day, it's your life, which means you'll need to get very comfortable trusting yourself. Doing things exactly as others have advised may solve a problem in the short term. But there won't always be someone beside you to show you the "correct" path. Trusting yourself means getting in touch with your gut. If you don't, it can slowly erode your confidence in finding solutions to other issues that will inevitably arise — which *will* happen, as the only true constant in parenting is change.

So trust your gut. Trust that even if you do not feel an instant bond with your baby, you will be able to form one — if you stay the course. Be brave enough to admit when you make mistakes. Because you will. And that's okay. Every parent does. The important thing is to learn from each one of them, and be better because of them. Again, the job of a parent is a lot of work, but it's also one of the most meaningful and fulfilling jobs you'll ever take on.

2) BUILD YOUR SUPPORT SYSTEM

I once read a story about an expectant dad who took to social media, voicing concerns over all of the negative comments and forewarnings he was receiving about becoming a parent. The response? Over 5,000 positive and uplifting messages of love and support.

You see, once you have a kid, you become part of a global community of parents. And like any massive community, some are gonna be haters. But on the whole, it's a wonderful community to be a part of. And one you should take full advantage of. It may take some time, but you *will* find your people to help you through any hurdles that may arise. A strong support system will assist you in being the best version of yourself for your impressionable little one — who will be looking to you as a model for their own emotional and intellectual development.

The benefits of building a reliable support system are undeniable... but only if you let down your guard and allow others in. Bottling up struggles benefits no one and will inevitably do more damage than good for the whole family.

Always take the time to share whatever you might be feeling (as there are many out there who have likely dealt with something similar), but also take the time to *listen*. There's a beautiful, nearly 2,000-year-old quote from the Talmud that translates to:

> "Who is wise? The one who learns from all."[1]

Not every story or piece of advice will apply, but stay open. You never know when you might find a tidbit that changes everything for the better.

Life as a new parent can feel isolating at times. But it goes by too quickly to waste a single moment. If you find yourself unhappy or something feels off, make the time to pause and figure out the problem. Whatever you are going through, I can guarantee that you are not the first… and you won't be the last. The most important thing to remember is that you are *not* alone.

Look after your mental health as much as you do your physical well-being. It's nearly impossible to be a strong and stable support system for your family when you are struggling. Lead by example if you want to raise a child you can be proud to call your own. And there is no better example that you can provide than asking for help when you need it.

3) FORM A UNITED FRONT WITH YOUR CO-PARENT

The key to almost any successful co-parenting relationship relies heavily on finding the right balance of shared responsibilities. It doesn't need to be a 50/50 split, nor does it need to be set in stone. But the sooner you get on the same page, the better your chances at weathering any storms that might come your way.

However, to build that united front, you must make the time to put systems and strategies in place to ensure you always have each other's back. Respect your Agreed-Upon Parameters with consistency, transparency, and follow-through. Share responsibilities while fully owning the mental load for whatever falls on your individual plate. Trust that your co-parent will have your back if and when you hit a breaking point and require a Freedom Shift. And be ready to do the same for them when needed.

Lastly, know that nurturing your connection with your co-parent (or yourself, for that matter) does not mean you're neglecting the needs of your child. Parenting is all about balancing priorities. And our children need to see that we have that same love and respect for ourselves as we do the other relationships in our lives.

In the end, the more you act as a connected team, the less confusing it will be for your kid — leaving them more room to enjoy their childhood rather than navigate the ups and downs of your relationship. And let's face it, the more connected you are with your co-parent, the more relaxed your home will be, and the more joy you'll find in your day-to-day lives.

YOUR INVOLVEMENT MATTERS

Women have been having babies for hundreds of thousands of years, and men have been right there beside them — experiencing many of the same feelings you may be feeling. And they survived. Thrived even.

On the DILF podcast, we've heard countless stories of dads who've found joy and transformed their kids' lives just by being present. But don't just trust me. Of the substantial research published since 1980 on father involvement and child well-being, 82% of these studies showed "significant associations between *positive* father involvement and offspring well-being."[2,3] Furthermore, over 100 studies on parent-child relationships show that having a loving and nurturing father is just as important for a child's happiness and mental well-being (as well as their social and academic success) as having a loving and nurturing mother. Study after study proves that our kids thrive when we show up. In short, your dedicated involvement matters.[4]

So as you enter this new world of parenthood, know that you will be presented with many choices on a daily basis that often come down to the same question: Do you want to follow old and outdated patterns on the homefront, or do you want to forge a new path as an actively-engaged,

MYTH #10 – YOU WILL LOVE *EVERY* MOMENT OF BEING A PARENT

emotionally-evolved, communicative member of your family (and society in general)?

The choice is yours… but remember, your children are watching. So choose wisely.

IN CONCLUSION

In the wise words of Brené Brown, "What we know matters, but who we are matters more."[5]

You now have a wide array of tools at your disposal — use them. Because you deserve to be happy and healthy, and so does your family. That's the ultimate goal of all of this, right?

And remember, as a great professor of mine used to say, "You control your own weather." In other words, there will always be highs and lows on the rollercoaster that is parenthood, but enjoying the ride will ultimately depend on you.

The final reminder I'll offer is to practice gratitude on a daily basis, as the things you are grateful for today are not guaranteed to be there tomorrow.

And with that, I'll leave you with one of my favorite quotes[6] — a sentiment that feels perfect for the start of any parenting adventure:

> "Enjoy the little things in life
> because one day you'll look back and realize…
> they were the BIG things."

QR RESOURCE GUIDE

THE DILF GLOSSARY

The following is a list of parenting terms for your reference. Some are well-known; some have been redefined, while others are newly-coined terms introduced in this book (designated with ⓓ).

- *Agreed-Upon Parameters*ⓓ > A short list of steadfast rules regarding your child and home, mutually agreed-upon by co-parents.

- *Birthing Parent* > A parent who physically gave birth to their child.

- *Box Breathing* > A controlled breathing exercise (also known as square breathing), renowned for its effectiveness in managing stress and anxiety. It is said to be based on pranayama, an ancient yoga practice originating in India. See Myth #5 with more detailed instructions.

- *Choose Your Battles* > A mindset that encourages one to pause and prioritize their time and energy in order to focus on what truly matters.

- *Co-Feeding* > When more than one individual takes on feeding responsibilities for a baby, regardless of the milk source.

- *Combination Feeding* (AKA mixed feeding) > When you feed your baby a mix of both breastmilk and infant formula.

- *Co-Parent* > A title earned by working together with at least one other individual in sharing the weight and responsibility of parenthood — regardless of your relationship status or living situation.

- *Co-Sleeping* > The practice of a caregiver (typically a parent) sleeping in the same bed or same room as a child.

- *Dadvocate* > One who advocates for the needs of a dad, and is vocal about actively ensuring dads are welcomed within the parenting space as an active member of the family unit.

- *Dedicated Observation* > The practice of regularly allowing yourself to be fully present with your child, while eliminating all distractions and taking note of how they respond to various environments and stimuli. The point of this practice is to make you an expert translator with regards to your child's preferences and needs.

- *Dream Feed* > A technique where you rouse your infant — without fully waking them — to do a night feed in order to attempt longer stretches of uninterrupted sleep.

- *Fourth Trimester* > The adjustment period for both parents and their baby during the first three months following the baby's birth.

- *Freedom Shift*® > Popularized by *The DILF (Dad I'd Like To Friend) Podcast*, this pre-arranged time period allows a parent the freedom to do whatever they see fit without any responsibility whatsoever.

- *Gatekeeping* > Often referred to as maternal gatekeeping, this is the tendency of one parent to control or restrict their partner's involvement regarding childcare and household responsibilities.

- *Invisible Support System*® > As opposed to a support system of friends and family, this term refers to resources like podcasts, books, inspiring playlists, or online communities — anywhere you can turn to if and when help is needed.

- *Learn Your Kid* ⒟ > Allowing the time and space to get to know *your* baby.

- *Mental Load* > The invisible weight that comes with all the behind-the-scenes cognitive and emotional work of managing one's life — from anticipating family needs and identifying solutions to coordinating schedules, organizing, and planning to keep a household running smoothly.

- *Mind-Calming Activities* > Pursuits that tend to rejuvenate you, and ultimately better your life — usually involving some form of "connection." For more details, see a list of potential activities within Myth #9.

- *Mind-Numbing Activities* > Diversions that may pass the time as a form of avoiding whatever is causing you stress, but rarely helping to relieve any of that stress.

- *Newborn Care Specialist (NCS)* > A professional trained in newborn care, hired to add additional support by focusing solely on the baby's needs. In the past, some used this term synonymously with "night nurse," but that's now considered outdated as a "night nurse" only refers to a NCS who is also a registered nurse.

- *Non-Birthing Parent* > An individual who became a parent through any method other than physically birthing their child: whether biologically related or not, including parents through surrogacy, marriage, or adoption.

- *Parental Leave* > A permitted work hiatus for *any* parent to bond with their baby and learn how to navigate this new world of parenthood.

- *Paternity Leave* > A crucial time period where fathers step away from work and their outside responsibilities in order to focus on bonding with their new arrival, supporting any potential co-parent, and adjusting to this next (extremely fulfilling) phase of life.

- *Perinatal* > The time period from conception and continuing up to roughly one year after birth — although some extend this period up to 24 months following the birth of a child.

- *Perinatal Mood and Anxiety Disorders (PMADs)* > An umbrella term that encompasses a range of mental health disorders affecting new and expectant parents. Although too-often undiagnosed, PMADs affect a significant proportion of new parents — whether or not they gave birth to their baby — impacting their emotional well-being and ability to cope with the challenges of parenthood.

- *Personal Boundaries* > The limits and rules individuals establish for themselves in order to define how they want to live their life and be treated by others.

- *Point of Calm*® > The limited time period when your little one is fully relaxed, but not yet asleep. And, in my opinion, the perfect time to exit the scene and empower your baby to dose off on their own.

- *Postpartum (AKA Postnatal)* > This term literally means "post-birth." It applies to the first six to eight weeks (approximately) following delivery of a newborn.

- *Postpartum Depression (PPD)* > A mood disorder following the birth of a baby, causing intense feelings of sadness, anxiety, or despair.

- *Postpartum Doula* > A trained professional hired to support a family during the postpartum period. As opposed to a NCS, this person typically focuses on the family as a whole and guides parents through recovery with newborn care and household support.

- *Prenatal* > The stage of pregnancy before a child is born.

- *Scope of Work (SOW)* > The list of tasks you've agreed to take full responsibility for — including any prep work associated with following a task through to completion.

- *Secure Attachment* > A term used to define a strong, healthy emotional bond between a child and their caregiver — whether biologically related or not. It's often characterized by a child feeling confident and comforted in that caregiver's presence, allowing them to explore their environment with a sense of safety and security.

- *Self-Care* > Actions taken to preserve or improve one's own health. See a list of potential mind-calming activities within Myth #9.

- *Skin-to-Skin Contact (SSC)* > The practice of placing a newborn baby — typically wearing only a diaper — directly on the bare chest of a parent (whether biologically related or not) in order to promote bonding as well as numerous other health advantages.

- *Support System* > A grouping of people and resources that provide mental, emotional and practical assistance and encouragement when needed. This can include a support network of your co-parent, friends, family, an in-person support group or a therapist. It can also include an Invisible Support System of resources like books, podcasts, and online communities — anywhere you can turn to during challenging times.

- *The Human Cradle*® > A technique used to bring a baby to the Point of Calm in preparation for sleep. It is based on the practice of *Alexander Technique* — a method of re-educating the body and mind to improve posture, coordination, tension relief and overall movement efficiency. See Myth #5 for more detailed instructions.

- *United Front* > A team-first mentality: working alongside your parenting partner to always be on the same page — supporting one another, even when you disagree.

- *Weekly Business Meeting (WBM)*® > A weekly check-in with your co-parent to reconnect, clear the air, and make plans for the week ahead.

ENDNOTES

Introduction

1. It's possible Mark Twain may not have actually said this, but the spirit of the sentiment still stands!
2. Tvtropes.org. "Bumbling Dad." *TV Tropes*, n.d. https://tvtropes.org/pmwiki/pmwiki.php/Main/BumblingDad.
3. TEDx Talks. "Good Dads — the Real Game Changer | Dr. Meg Meeker | TEDxTraverseCity." *YouTube*, October 15, 2014. https://www.youtube.com/watch?v=pQ3Dkrt-8O4&list=PLImGq9mWKHbPPp48S7WeIhK_MLFUxMSD8&index=2.

Myth #1

1. Rachel Minkin and Juliana Horowitz. "1. Gender and Parenting." *Pew Research Center's Social & Demographic Trends Project*, January 24, 2023. https://www.pewresearch.org/social-trends/2023/01/24/gender-and-parenting/.

ENDNOTES

2. Bahar Gholipour. "5 Ways Fatherhood Changes a Man's Brain." *Live Science,* June 14, 2014. https://www.livescience.com/46322-fatherhood-changes-brain.html.
3. Anna Machin. *The Life of Dad: The Making of a Modern Father.* Simon & Schuster, 2018, 78.
4. Alison Wood Brooks. "Get Excited: Reappraising Pre-Performance Anxiety as Excitement." *Journal of Experimental Psychology: General 143,* no. 3 (June 2014): 1144–58. https://doi.org/10.1037/a0035325.
5. Svetlana Whitener. "Council Post: Anxiety vs. Relaxation: Relabeling Anxiety as Excitement." *Forbes,* August 12, 2024. https://www.forbes.com/councils/forbescoachescouncil/2021/04/07/anxiety-vs-relaxationrelabeling-anxiety-as-excitement/.
6. Courtney Pierce Keeton, Maureen Perry-Jenkins, and Aline G. Sayer. "Sense of Control Predicts Depressive and Anxious Symptoms across the Transition to Parenthood." *Journal of Family Psychology 22,* no. 2 (2008): 212–221. https://doi.org/10.1037/0893-3200.22.2.212.
7. Nehal Aggarwal. "The Benefits of Talking to Baby in Utero." *The Bump,* July 29, 2024. https://www.thebump.com/a/talking-to-baby-in-utero.
8. Amy Morin. "7 Scientifically Proven Benefits of Gratitude." *Psychology Today.* April 3, 2015. https://www.psychologytoday.com/us/blog/what-mentally-strong-people-dont-do/201504/7-scientifically-proven-benefits-of-gratitude.
9. Monique Haicault. "La Gestion Ordinaire de La Vie En Deux." *Sociologie Du Travail 26, no.3* (1984): 268–277. https://doi.org/10.3406/sotra.1984.2072.
10. Tova B. Walsh, Emma Carpenter, Molly A. Costanzo, Lanikque Howard, and Rachel Reynders. "Present as a Partner and a Parent: Mothers' and Fathers' Perspectives on Father Participation in

Prenatal Care." *Infant Mental Health Journal 42, no. 3* (May 5, 2021). https://doi.org/10.1002/imhj.21920.

11. Kevin Seldon. "Reimagining Fatherhood." Podcast. *The DILF (Dad I'd Like To Friend) Podcast*, July 30, 2020. https://dadidliketofriend.com/reimagining-fatherhood-dilfs-dadvocate-series/.

12. Natasha J. Cabrera, Jay Fagan, and Danielle Farrie. "Explaining the Long Reach of Fathers' Prenatal Involvement on Later Paternal Engagement." *Journal of Marriage and Family 70, no. 5* (December 2008): 1094–1107. https://doi.org/10.1111/j.1741-3737.2008.00551.x.

13. ManSoo Yu, Jane A. McElory, Linda F.C. Bullock, and Kevin D. Everett. "Unique Perspectives of Women and Their Partners Using the Prenatal Psychosocial Profile Scale." *Journal of Advanced Nursing 67, no. 8* (March 28, 2011): 1767–78. https://doi.org/10.1111/j.1365-2648.2011.05628.x.

14. Kevin Shafer. "Why Dads Can't Be the Dads They Want to Be." *The Conversation*, May 11, 2017. https://theconversation.com/why-dads-cant-be-the-dads-they-want-to-be-75045.

15. Daniel Cox. "American Men Suffer a Friendship Recession." *The Survey Center on American Life*, July 6, 2021. https://www.americansurveycenter.org/commentary/american-men-suffer-a-friendship-recession/.

16. Kevin Seldon. "Modern Dadhood." Podcast. *The DILF (Dad I'd Like To Friend) Podcast*, March 12, 2020. https://dadidliketofriend.com/modern-dadhood/.

17. Pope Francis. "Catechesis on Saint Joseph - 6. Saint Joseph, Jesus' Foster Father." Presented at the General Audience, January 5, 2022. https://www.vatican.va/content/francesco/en/audiences/2022/documents/20220105-udienza-generale.html.

Myth #2

1. Gwynn Guilford. "More Workers Take Parental Leave as States, Employers Expand Eligibility." *Wall Street Journal*, April 8, 2023. https://www.wsj.com/articles/more-workers-take-parental-leave-as-states-employers-expand-eligibility-8eaf8e3a.

2. *This concept is further explored in the following*: Maggie Wooll. "Paternity Leave in the US: A Guide to Getting It Right." *BetterUp*, April 6, 2022. https://www.betterup.com/blog/paternity-leave-in-the-us.

3. *This concept is further explored in the following*: The Economist. "The Benefits of Paternity Leave," *The Economist*, May 14, 2015. https://www.economist.com/the-economist-explains/2015/05/14/the-benefits-of-paternity-leave.

4. Tim Allen. "I'm a CEO and a Working Dad. Here's What I Wish I Did Differently." *Harvard Business Review*, December 8, 2020. https://hbr.org/2020/12/im-a-ceo-and-a-working-dad-heres-what-i-wish-i-did-differently.

5. Wyndi Kappes. "Study: Providing Parents with Support Makes Businesses More Profitable." *The Bump*, March 20, 2024. https://www.thebump.com/news/parents-more-productive-workers#.

6. Joseph Fuller. "Healthy Outcomes: How Employers' Support for Employees with Caregiving Responsibilities Can Benefit the Organization." *The Project on Workforce*. Harvard Business School, July 22, 2022. https://www.hbs.edu/ris/Publication%20Files/Healthy%20Outcomes%20Report_9886821c-213d-481c-94c1-ddb8eae134bf.pdf.

7. Richard J. Petts, Chris Knoester, and Jane Waldfogel. "Fathers' Paternity Leave-Taking and Children's Perceptions of Father-Child Relationships in the United States." *Sex Roles 82*, no. 1 (May 4, 2019). https://doi.org/10.1007/s11199-019-01050-y.

8. T. Gupta, G. Barker, and C. Lewis. "State of American Men 2025." *Equimundo: Center for Masculinities and Social Justice*, 2025. https://www.equimundo.org/wp-content/uploads/2025/06/State-of-American-Men-2025.pdf

9. Jack Kelly. "The Rise of the Stay-At-Home Dad." *Forbes*, December 7, 2022. https://www.forbes.com/sites/jackkelly/2022/12/07/the-rise-of-the-stay-at-home-dad/.

10. Gretchen Livingston. "Growing Number of Dads Home with the Kids: Biggest Increase among Those Caring for Family." *Pew Research Center's Social and Demographic Trends Project*, June 5, 2014. https://www.pewresearch.org/social-trends/wp-content/uploads/sites/3/2014/06/2014-06-05_Stay-at-Home-Dads.pdf.

11. Darby Saxbe and Sofia Cardenas. "What Paternity Leave Does for a Father's Brain." *The New York Times*, November 8, 2021. https://www.nytimes.com/2021/11/08/opinion/paid-family-leave-fathers.html.

12. Richard J. Petts, Daniel L. Carlson, and Chris Knoester. "If I [Take] Leave, Will You Stay? Paternity Leave and Relationship Stability." *Journal of Social Policy 49*, no. 4 (November 14, 2019): 1–21. https://doi.org/10.1017/s0047279419000928.

13. Xiao Xiao and Alice Yuen Loke. "The Effects of Co-Parenting / Intergenerational Co-Parenting Interventions during the Postpartum Period: A Systematic Review." *International Journal of Nursing Studies 119* (April 2021). https://doi.org/10.1016/j.ijnurstu.2021.103951.

14. Nathaniel Popper. "What Baby Formula Does for Fathers." *The New York Times*, February 23, 2019. https://www.nytimes.com/2019/02/23/opinion/sunday/formula-breastfeeding-fatherhood.html.

15. Anamarija Brnjarchevska and Zenger News. "Two-Thirds of New Dads Feel 'Left Out' in the Early Days of Parenting." *Newsweek*, April 26, 2022. https://www.newsweek.com/two-thirds-new-dads-feel-left-out-early-days-parenting-1701107.

16. Brnjarchevska and Zenger News, "Two-Thirds of New Dads Feel 'Left Out' in the Early Days of Parenting."
17. Brnjarchevska and Zenger News, "Two-Thirds of New Dads Feel 'Left Out' in the Early Days of Parenting."
18. *This quote has been attributed to Churchill, but there is no definitive source to prove it.*

Myth #3

1. Lucy Notarantonio. "Man Divides Opinion for What He Said to Fiancee Right after She Gave Birth." *Newsweek,* July 5, 2024. https://www.newsweek.com/man-divides-opinions-what-he-said-fiancee-after-birth-1921593.
2. The Telegraph Men. "New Fathers Struggle to Bond with Their Children due to 'Maternal Gatekeeping.'" *The Telegraph,* May 19, 2015. https://www.telegraph.co.uk/men/relationships/fatherhood/11614742/New-fathers-struggle-to-bond-with-their-children-due-to-maternal-gatekeeping.html.
3. The Telegraph Men. "New Fathers Struggle to Bond with Their Children due to 'Maternal Gatekeeping.'"
4. Anamarija Brnjarchevska and Zenger News. "Two-Thirds of New Dads Feel 'Left Out' in the Early Days of Parenting." *Newsweek,* April 26, 2022. https://www.newsweek.com/two-thirds-new-dads-feel-left-out-early-days-parenting-1701107.
5. Michael E. Lamb. "Mothers, Fathers, Families, and Circumstances: Factors Affecting Children's Adjustment." *Applied Developmental Science 16,* no. 2 (2012): 98-111. https://doi.org/10.1080/10888691.2012.667344.
6. Er-Mei Chen, Meei-Ling Gau, Chieh-Yu Liu, and Tzu-Ying Lee. "Effects of Father-Neonate Skin-To-Skin Contact on Attachment: A Randomized Controlled Trial." *Nursing Research and Practice*

7. Alyssa R. Morris, Alexandra Turner, Chase H. Gilbertson, Geoffrey Corner, Armando J. Mendez, and Darby E. Saxbe. "Physical Touch during Father-Infant Interactions Is Associated with Paternal Oxytocin Levels." *Infant Behavior and Development* 64 (August 2021): 101613. https://doi.org/10.1016/j.infbeh.2021.101613.

8. caringforkids.cps.ca. "Read, Speak, Sing to Your Baby: How Parents Can Promote Literacy from Birth," *Caring for Kids*, March 2022. https://caringforkids.cps.ca/handouts/behavior-and-development/read_speak_sing_to_your_baby.

9. AWHONN. "Father's Day: A Father's Bond with His Newborn Is Just as Important as a Mother's Bond." *AWHONN*, October 23, 2019. https://www.awhonn.org/fathers-day-a-fathers-bond-with-his-newborn-is-just-as-important-as-a-mothers-bond/.

10. AWHONN. "Father's Day: A Father's Bond with His Newborn Is Just as Important as a Mother's Bond."

11. Kendra Cherry, MSEd. "How Attachment Theory Works." *Verywell Mind*, January 29, 2025. https://www.verywellmind.com/what-is-attachment-theory-2795337

Myth #4

1. Mayo Clinic. "Postpartum Depression - Symptoms and Causes." *Mayo Clinic*, November 24, 2022. https://www.mayoclinic.org/diseases-conditions/postpartum-depression/symptoms-causes/syc-20376617.

2. OASH. "Postpartum Depression | Office on Women's Health." *womenshealth.gov*, October 17, 2023. https://womenshealth.gov/mental-health/mental-health-conditions/postpartum-depression.

3. *More Myths Surrounding PPD can be found in the following:*

ENDNOTES

    Psych Central. "Postpartum Depression: 6 Myths," *Psych Central,* January 13, 2022. https://psychcentral.com/depression/5-damaging-myths-about-postpartum-depression#may-cause-harm-to-baby.

4. Postpartum Support Virginia. "Perinatal Mood and Anxiety Disorders (PMADs)." *Postpartum Support Virginia,* n.d. https://postpartumva.org/types-of-perinatal-mood-and-anxiety-disorders/.

5. Pilyoung Kim and James Swain. "Sad Dads: Paternal Postpartum Depression." *Psychiatry 2007* (2007): 35–47. https://pmc.ncbi.nlm.nih.gov/articles/PMC2922346/pdf/PE_4_2_36.pdf.

6. Cleveland Clinic. "Yes, Postpartum Depression in Men Is Very Real." *Cleveland Clinic Health Essentials.* n.d. https://health.clevelandclinic.org/yes-postpartum-depression-in-men-is-very-real.

7. *Medical News Today.* "Men's Testosterone Drops Steeply When Baby Arrives." *Medical News Today,* September 13, 2011. https://www.medicalnewstoday.com/articles/234266#1.

8. Magdalena Martínez-García, María Paternina-Die, Sofia I Cardenas, Oscar Vilarroya, Manuel Desco, Susanna Carmona, and Darby E Saxbe. "First-Time Fathers Show Longitudinal Gray Matter Cortical Volume Reductions: Evidence from Two International Samples." *Cerebral Cortex 33, no. 7* (September 7, 2022). https://doi.org/10.1093/cercor/bhac333.

9. UT Southwestern Medical Center. "1 in 10 Dads Experience Postpartum Depression, Anxiety: How to Spot the Signs." *UT Southwestern Medical Center,* August 17, 2021. https://utswmed.org/medblog/paternal-postpartum-depression/.

10. Kim Hooper. "I Gave Birth, but My Husband Developed Postpartum Depression." *The New York Times,* July 19, 2021. https://www.nytimes.com/2021/07/19/well/mind/men-postpartum-depression.html.

11. James F. Paulson, and Sharnail D. Bazemore. "Prenatal and Postpartum Depression in Fathers and Its Association with Maternal Depression." *JAMA 303, no. 19* (May 19, 2010): 1961–69. https://doi.org/10.1001/jama.2010.605.

12. Tova B. Walsh, R. Neal Davis, Craig Garfield. "A Call to Action: Screening Fathers for Perinatal Depression." *Pediatrics, vol. 145,1* (January 2020): e20191193. https://doi.org/10.1542/peds.2019-1193

13. DaddiLife. "The Rise of the Modern Day Dad – Alternadads and Overcoming Barriers." *DaddiLife,* October 28, 2016. https://www.daddilife.com/heroes/modern-day-dad/rise-modern-day-dad-alternadads-overcoming-barriers/

14. Sheehan D. Fisher. "Paternal Mental Health: Why Is It Relevant?" *American Journal of Lifestyle Medicine 11, no. 3* (February 16, 2016): 200–211. https://doi.org/10.1177/1559827616629895.

15. UT Southwestern Medical Center. "1 in 10 Dads Experience Postpartum Depression, Anxiety: How to Spot the Signs." *UT Southwestern Medical Center,* August 17, 2021. https://utswmed.org/medblog/paternal-postpartum-depression/.

16. Jonathan Scarff. "Postpartum Depression in Men." *Innovations in Clinical Neuroscience,* May 2019. https://pmc.ncbi.nlm.nih.gov/articles/PMC6659987/pdf/icns_16_5-6_11.pdf.

17. Will Courtenay. "Helping Men Beat the Baby Blues and Overcome Depression." *PostpartumMen,* 2008. https://postpartummen.com/postpartum-depression/.

18. Genevieve Le Bas, Stephanie R. Aarsman, Alana Rogers, Jacqui A. Macdonald, Gessica Misuraca, Sarah Khor, Elizabeth A. Spry, et al. "Paternal Perinatal Depression, Anxiety, and Stress and Child Development." *JAMA Pediatrics,* June 16, 2025. https://doi.org/10.1001/jamapediatrics.2025.0880.

19. Massachusetts General Hospital and Harvard Medical School. "Harvard Second Generation Study." *Harvard Second Generation Study,* 2015. https://www.adultdevelopmentstudy.org/.

20. Robert Waldinger. "What Makes a Good Life? Lessons from the Longest Study on Happiness." *Ted.com*. TED Talks, November 2015. https://www.ted.com/talks/robert_waldinger_what_makes_a_good_life_lessons_from_the_longest_study_on_happiness.

Myth #5

1. A Freedom Shift is a concept I coined in 2020 while working on The DILF Podcast. It was later featured in the following article: Marisa LaScala. "The Myth of the Primary Parent." *Good Housekeeping*, March 1, 2023. https://www.goodhousekeeping.com/life/parenting/a45156375/myth-of-the-primary-parent.

2. Dan Puglisi. "Babies Sense Parents' Emotions to Help Understand Their World." *First Things First,* August 31, 2017. https://www.firstthingsfirst.org/first-things/babies-sense-parents-emotions-help-understand-world/.

3. MIT. "The Internet Classics Archive: The Discourses by Epictetus." *The Internet Classics Archive | The Discourses by Epictetus, n.d., 2.5.4–5.* https://classics.mit.edu/Epictetus/discourses.html

4. Howard E LeWine. "Understanding the Stress Response." *Harvard Health Publishing*, 2024. https://www.health.harvard.edu/staying-healthy/understanding-the-stress-response.

5. WebMD. "What Is Box Breathing?" *WebMD*, April 25, 2025. https://www.webmd.com/balance/what-is-box-breathing.

6. Gretchen Cuda. "Just Breathe: Body Has a Built-in Stress Reliever." *NPR.org*, 2019. https://www.npr.org/2010/12/06/131734718/just-breathe-body-has-a-built-in-stress-reliever.

7. Childrens.com. "Know When to Talk to Your Pediatrician about Your Child's Development." *Children's Health,* 2017. https://www.childrens.com/health-wellness/know-when-to-talk-to-your-pediatrician-about-your-childs-development.

8. Edzard Ernst. "Alternative Medicine – A Critical Assessment of 150 Modalities." *Springer Cham* (2019): 153–154. https://doi.org/10.1007/978-3-031-10710-8.

9. Diane Bales. "Creating Consistency to Aid Brain Development in Babies." *Field Report,* Athens, GA: University of Georgia College of Agricultural and Environmental Sciences, September 1, 2014. https://fieldreport.caes.uga.edu/publications/C1053-11/creating-consistency-to-aid-brain-development-in-babies/#:~:text=The%20developing%20brain%20thrives%20on,take%20care%20of%20his%20needs.

10. National Heart, Lung, and Blood Institute. "What Are Sleep Deprivation and Deficiency?" *National Heart, Lung, and Blood Institute,* March 24, 2022. https://www.nhlbi.nih.gov/health/sleep-deprivation.

Myth #6

1. Ivanhoe Newswire. "New Research Shows Mistakes May Actually Be Key to Learning: Remote Learning Has Amplified Problem for Some Students." *KSAT,* June 1, 2021. https://www.ksat.com/news/local/2021/06/01/new-research-shows-mistakes-may-actually-be-key-to-learning/.

2. Arlin Cuncic. "The Psychology of Shame." *Verywellmind,* May 27, 2021. https://www.verywellmind.com/what-is-shame-5115076.

3. Dan Santat. *After the Fall: How Humpty Dumpty Got Back up Again.* New York: Roaring Brook Press, 2017.

4. Lisa Fletcher. "The Good Way to Fight." *Cincinnati Family Magazine*, April 8, 2024. https://cincinnatifamilymagazine.com/the-good-way-to-fight/.
5. Lisa Fletcher. "The Good Way to Fight."
6. Sarah M. Allen and Alan J. Hawkins. "Maternal Gatekeeping: Mothers' Beliefs and Behaviors That Inhibit Greater Father Involvement in Family Work." *Journal of Marriage and the Family* 61, no. 1 (February 1999): 199. https://doi.org/10.2307/353894.
7. Elissa Strauss. "Maternal Gatekeeping: Why Moms Don't Let Dads Help." *CNN*, December 6, 2017. https://www.cnn.com/2017/12/06/health/maternal-gatekeeping-strauss/index.html.
8. Shannon Carpenter. *The Ultimate Stay-At-Home Dad: Your Essential Manual for Being an Awesome Full-Time Father*. New York: Penguin Books, 2021.
9. Samuel Beckett. *Worstward Ho*. New York: Grove Press Inc, 1983.

Myth #7

1. Familydoctor.org. "Recovering from Delivery - Postpartum Recovery." *Familydoctor.org,* January 26, 2017. https://familydoctor.org/recovering-from-delivery/.
2. Mayo Clinic. "Sex after Pregnancy: Set Your Own Timeline." *Mayo Clinic,* March 26, 2024. https://www.mayoclinic.org/healthy-lifestyle/labor-and-delivery/in-depth/sex-after-pregnancy/art-20045669.
3. David Olson, Amy Olson-Sigg, and Peter Larson. "National Survey of Married Couples." *Life Innovations, Inc.*, 2011. https://www.prepare-enrich.com/wp-content/uploads/2020/12/national_survey_married.pdf.

4. *We discuss the topic of "Happy Wife, Happy Life" in detail in the following:*

   "When You're All Tapped Out | Beleaf in Fatherhood." Podcast. Dad I'd Like To Friend (The DILF Podcast), May 20, 2021. https://dadidliketofriend.com/when-youre-all-tapped-out-beleaf-in-fatherhood/.

5. Emma Seppälä. "The Science behind the Joy of Sharing Joy." *Psychology Today,* July 15, 2013. https://www.psychologytoday.com/us/blog/feeling-it/201307/the-science-behind-the-joy-sharing-joy.

6. Kevin Seldon. "Acknowledgement (DILF's Co-Parenting Series)." Podcast. *Dad I'd Like To Friend (The DILF Podcast),* February 20, 2020. https://dadidliketofriend.com/acknowledgement-dilfs-co-parenting-series/

7. David Olson, Amy Olson-Sigg, and Peter Larson. "National Survey of Married Couples." *Life Innovations, Inc.,* 2011. https://www.prepare-enrich.com/wp-content/uploads/2020/12/national_survey_married.pdf.

8. Jasmine Zhang, Sheri Madigan, and Dillon Browne. "Caregivers' Psychological Distress, Technology Use, and Parenting: The Importance of a Multidimensional Perspective." *Computers in Human Behavior 134* (September 1, 2022): 107324. https://doi.org/10.1016/j.chb.2022.107324.

9. Claire McCarthy. "Room Sharing with Your Baby May Help Prevent SIDS, but It Means Everyone Gets Less Sleep." *Harvard Health,* June 6, 2017. https://www.health.harvard.edu/blog/room-sharing-with-your-baby-may-help-prevent-sids-but-it-means-everyone-gets-less-sleep-201706062525.

10. Sofia Lodato. "Hugs Impact Your Brain and Mental Health." *Oprah Daily,* May 15, 2025. https://www.oprahdaily.com/life/health/a64706694/hugs-impact-brain-mental-health/.

11. Massachusetts General Hospital, and Harvard Medical School. "Harvard Second Generation Study." *Harvard Second Generation Study*, 2015. https://www.adultdevelopmentstudy.org/.

12. Xiao Xiao, and Alice Yuen Loke. "The Effects of Co-Parenting / Intergenerational Co-Parenting Interventions during the Postpartum Period: A Systematic Review." *International Journal of Nursing Studies 119* (April 2021). https://doi.org/10.1016/j.ijnurstu.2021.103951.

Myth #8

1. John Medina. Brain Rules for Baby How to Raise a Smart and Happy Child from Zero to Five. Seattle Pear, 2014, p. 65.

2. Simone Davies. "Everything You Need to Know about Montessori Observation and Why It's Helpful." The Montessori Notebook, November 4, 2019. https://themontessorinotebook.com/everything-you-need-to-know-about-montessori-observation.

3. Connor Garel. "A Rookie Guide to How Dads Can Help with Newborns." HuffPost, July 19, 2019. https://www.huffpost.com/archive/ca/entry/how-dads-can-help-with-newborns_ca_5d321dfee4b020cd9943776e.

4. Kevin Seldon. "Living Adventurously… With Kids | Johnnyswim." Podcast. The DILF (Dad I'd Like To Friend) Podcast, August 5, 2021. https://dadidliketofriend.com/living-adventurously-with-kids-johnnyswim/.

5. Brene Brown. "The Anatomy of Trust." Lecture presented at the SuperSoul Sessions, November 1, 2015. https://brenebrown.com/videos/anatomy-trust-video/.

Myth #9

1. Kevin Seldon. "What Doesn't Kill Us, Makes Us Stronger." Podcast. *The DILF (Dad I'd Like To Friend) Podcast,* September 2, 2021. https://dadidliketofriend.com/what-doesnt-kill-us-makes-us-stronger-dave-callaham/.

2. Marcel Schwantes. "Psychologist Adam Grant Says Your Overall Success at Work Comes Down to 3 Familiar Words." *Inc,* May 16, 2024. https://www.inc.com/marcel-schwantes/adam-grant-explains-success-comes-down-to-three-words.html.

3. Brene Brown. *Power of Vulnerability: Teachings on Authenticity, Connection, and Courage.* Sounds True, 2012.

4. Joel Bobby. "Mental Health Benefits of Coloring." *Mayo Clinic Health System,* August 15, 2022. https://www.mayoclinichealthsystem.org/hometown-health/speaking-of-health/coloring-is-good-for-your-health.

5. Vivek Murthy. "Parents under Pressure: The U.S. Surgeon General's Advisory on the Mental Health & Well-Being of Parents." Department of Health & Human Services. Washington D.C.: HHS, 2024. https://www.hhs.gov/sites/default/files/parents-under-pressure.pdf.

Myth #10

1. *Attributed to Ben Zoma in the following:* Pirkei Avot 4:1, in *The Talmud: A Reference Guide,* translated by Adin Steinsaltz (New York: Random House, 1989), 125.

2. Anna Sarkadi, Robert Kristiansson, Frank Oberklaid, and Sven Bremberg. "Fathers' Involvement and Children's Developmental Outcomes: A Systematic Review of Longitudinal Studies." *Acta Paediatrica 97,* no. 2 (February 2008): 153–158. https://doi.org/10.1111/j.1651-2227.2007.00572.x.

3. Paul R. Amato and Fernando Rivera. "Paternal Involvement and Children's Behavior Problems." *Journal of Marriage and Family* 61, no. 2 (1999): 375–384. https://doi.org/10.2307/353755.

4. Focus on the Family. "The Significance of a Father's Influence." *Focus on the Family,* 2011. https://www.focusonthefamily.com/family-qa/the-significance-of-a-fathers-influence/.

5. Brené Brown. *Daring Greatly: How the Courage to Be Vulnerable Transforms the Way We Live, Love, Parent, and Lead.* New York: Gotham Books, 2012, 15.

6. The origin of this quote is up for debate, but it seems to have been said by one Robert Brault.

ABOUT THE AUTHOR

KEVIN SELDON is a father, husband, and founder of a leading brand strategy consultancy within the social impact space. His clients have ranged from Fortune 500 companies and award-winning artists to world-renowned nonprofits. However, after five years of struggling to fulfill a lifelong dream of starting a family, he was left a bit broken. So, when he and his wife finally found themselves expecting, he took an extended hiatus from the firm he founded to better support his growing family and bond with his newborn son. He expected the experience to be exhilarating yet exhausting, but was shocked at the lack of support available to dads who seemed to be completely excluded from parenting culture.

ABOUT THE AUTHOR

In response to the isolation he felt, he created the celebrated parenting podcast, DILF (as in: Dad I'd Like To… FRIEND). Kevin's work with DILF has since been featured everywhere from *People Magazine* to *The New York Times*. What began as a simple forum to build a support network of dads Kevin would want to… friend, has evolved into a nonprofit called Dads Supporting Dads with one of the largest dad communities in the United States.

Kevin resides in Los Angeles, CA with his beautiful wife and son, who taught him that the best things in life… are worth the wait.

Thank you for taking the time to read this book.

If you enjoyed it, please consider writing a review to encourage other new dads to check it out:

www.ingramcontent.com/pod-product-compliance
Lightning Source LLC
Chambersburg PA
CBHW052136070526
44585CB00017B/1856